CH00749926

The Great Billy Butlin Race

THE FIRST AND ONLY FOOTRACE FROM JOHN O'GROATS TO LAND'S END

Robin Richards

Stairwell Books //

Published by Stairwell Books
161 Lowther Street
York, YO31 7LZ

www.stairwellbooks.co.uk
@stairwellbooks

ISBN: 978-1-913432-08-9

To all weary footsloggers who doggedly trek between John O'Groats and Land's End.

'Let the people march.'

Sir Billy Butlin

The Route from John O'Groats to Land's End

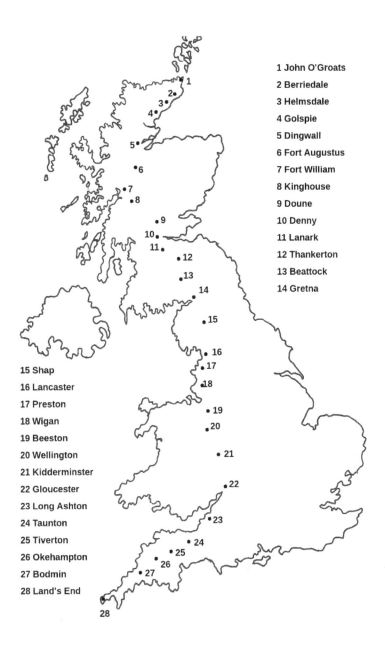

1 John O'Groats
2 Berriedale
3 Helmsdale
4 Golspie
5 Dingwall
6 Fort Augustus
7 Fort William
8 Kinghouse
9 Doune
10 Denny
11 Lanark
12 Thankerton
13 Beattock
14 Gretna

15 Shap
16 Lancaster
17 Preston
18 Wigan
19 Beeston
20 Wellington
21 Kidderminster
22 Gloucester
23 Long Ashton
24 Taunton
25 Tiverton
26 Okehampton
27 Bodmin
28 Land's End

Table of Contents

Chapter One: 'The Death Trek'

BY TEN THIRTY THAT NIGHT both men were soaked, chilled to the core and teetering on the brink of exhaustion. The springy and purposeful pace, which had stood them in good stead for more than 800 miles, had been reduced to something more like an old man's shuffle.

The wild expanses of Cornwall's Bodmin Moor on a bleak night in March is no place for the faint hearted. For those two men on that desolate night only the cold, the driving rain, their aching leg muscles and the road, a dark ribbon of tarmac which seemed to stretch endlessly before them, felt real.

The year was 1960 and they were racing for the honour of being the winner of the first, and indeed the *only* Great Billy Butlin Race. An event opposed by the Chief Constable of Caithness, the Secretary of State for Scotland and by the UK Parliament itself. A race dubbed by some tabloid newspapers as, 'The Death Trek?' A race for the honour of winning, that and a cheque for £1,000.

Billed as a footrace for the masses, run, walk or crawl, it didn't matter how you got there as long as it was on your own two legs. A dash for glory of almost one thousand miles, starting from the far north of Scotland at John O'Groats and slicing diagonally across the United Kingdom to the rocky peninsular of Land's End on the very tip of Cornwall. The longest trek you could make in Britain without doubling back on yourself. And all in the depths of a British winter.

Both runners were surprisingly similar in appearance and neither conformed to the conventional image of an athlete. These were not the rangy greyhounds of the sprint track, nor the loose-limbed distance runners most often seen on Olympic courses. These were men built for endurance rather than speed. Small, compact, powerful, and both from the north of England. There the similarity ended. John Grundy, a lorry driver from Wakefield in West Yorkshire, was at twenty-six the younger of the two. He had built a reputation over the years as one of England's finest and toughest marathon runners.

The second man, Jimmy Musgrave, a glass packer from Dunscroft near Doncaster was deemed by some to be the race's wild-card. At thirty-eight, the cloth-capped Musgrave was considered by many to be too old to be a serious contender, and lacked the racing pedigree of his rival. He himself had been quite dismissive of his own experience, claiming to have only ever raced in the occasional merchant seaman's event of four or five miles.

Grundy, dressed for marathon running in white shorts and singlet, gloves being his only concession to the atrocious weather, had been the race leader from the off, covering the first twenty miles from John O'Groats in a mere two hours and twenty minutes. Over the next eight hundred miles he disputed the lead with more than a dozen athletes and despite injuries, knocks and set-backs he left them all trailing in his wake. He was close behind the leaders when he crossed the border into England and throughout the race he was never more than a few miles from the front. As he approached Cornwall he had constantly outpaced his rivals, with the exception of one man, little Jimmy Musgrave.

Despite Musgrave's apparent lack of racing experience and being considered by many as the race's dark horse, he had entered the contest with a tactical plan in mind. He aimed to be in fifth place as he crossed the border and then gradually move up the field as they raced through the Midlands. Once in the West Country he planned to move into the lead and make a dash for the finish. It was a good plan and it worked in every aspect except one, it didn't take into account the cold and the energy sapping wilds of Bodmin Moor.

As darkness fell and the weather closed in, Grundy played a waiting game. There were still more than fifty miles to the winning post and Musgrave, maintaining a strong pace, had stretched out a lead of ten miles. This was where Grundy's marathon experience came into play. He was well aware of his own abilities. He knew when to push the pace and when to just jog along and bide his time. Musgrave, he was convinced, would never be able to maintain his blistering rate all the way to Land's End. He would be sure to burn out and be forced to stop and rest. Once Musgrave stopped, that would be all the opportunity John Grundy needed. He would surge ahead, take the lead and race on to the winning post where the race sponsor Mr Billy Butlin[1], holiday camp magnate and one of the richest men in Britain, would be waiting for him with a cheque for £1,000.

But Jim Musgrave had not read the script and he just kept on going.

When the crisis came and legs finally gave out, it affected both men at almost exactly the same time. Grundy, who had been gaining ground steadily, collapsed exhausted some three miles short of the planned rest stop. He couldn't go on any further, he told his support team, and he staggered out of the weather into the nearest shelter, a local pub.

While Grundy, wrapped in a blanket, shivered by the fire the customers and pub staff swung into action. People across Britain had taken the race to their hearts and generous and impromptu help for competitors had become common. The barmaid hung his kit up to dry in front of the fire and one of the regulars quickly drained his pint and went home to run Grundy a hot bath while his wife prepared some food.

The limited communications technology which existed in 1960 meant the flow of race information was very restricted. Both the Grundy and the Musgrave camp had to rely on word of mouth from spectators and reporters for their intelligence as to how the other competitors were fairing, and on that wild night on Bodmin Moor there were precious few of these around. Even Chris Brasher, reporting on the race for *The Guardian*, had been glad to file his last story, climb into a warm car and head for home.

When John Grundy collapsed into the pub, Jim Musgrave's effort ground to a halt a mere two hundred yards further along the road. His sturdy body was wracked with cramps and he keeled over onto the grass by the side of the road. 'I'm done,' he said, 'I can't go any further.' His backup team gently led him to a campervan parked by the roadside and set to work massaging his cramps. This was surely the end of his race.

It was at this point the Musgrave camp had an astonishing slice of luck. Through the wind and the rain one of Jim Musgrave's four-man

[1] Billy Butlin MBE did not become *Sir* Billy Butlin until 1964 when he was knighted by the Queen.

support team spotted John Grundy as he staggered along the road being helped from the pub to the bungalow where his hot bath was waiting. Withdrawing into the gloom he dashed back to the campervan and told them the news; Grundy was close and temporarily out of action. The effect on Musgrave was electrifying. He shrugged off the effects of the cramps, climbed back to his feet and was soon pacing down the road again, reinvigorated and intent once more on being the first man to reach Land's End.

By the time Grundy, fed and rested, was back on the road, Musgrave had extended his lead to five miles. It was a tall order, but marathon runner John Grundy was a competitor to the core, undaunted, he set off in pursuit.

THE COURAGE AND ENDURANCE OF John Grundy, Jim Musgrave and more than seven hundred other weary footsloggers who raced from John O'Groats to Land's End during that wild winter of 1960 have been largely forgotten. The race was unofficial, at least from the point of view of the middle-aged men in blazers who control national and international sport. A one-off race organised by a wealthy entrepreneur to meet a perceived public demand. A publicity stunt, some called it. The Amateur Athletics Association responded by stripping the amateur status from any athlete who took part in the Butlin Race rendering them ineligible to compete in the Olympic Games or any other national or international athletics event. John Grundy, Alf Rozentals, and the national women's walking champion Beryl Randle all lost their amateur status this way.

The nationwide craze for mammoth footraces flared brightly for just a few months in the latter part of 1959 and early 1960, holding the nation in thrall, delighting spectators, sports fans and newspaper readers, and creating a cheerful distraction from the usual gloomy winter news. Then, with the coming of spring and the exciting new trends of the decade which would soon come to be known as the 'Swinging Sixties', it faded away as crazes always do, leaving nothing but a memory or two, a few blisters, and some old newspaper photographs fading to yellow.

National crazes are, by their very nature, unpredictable, spontaneous and short-lived. Who can say why leg-warmers, space hoppers and the Rubik's cube took off as they did while other products, toys, diets, and

4

fads did not. Psychologists say there is within us all an inborn urge to follow a new trend or craze, to conform with our own tribe and not to be left behind by the pack.

If the new craze for marathon walking could be laid at anyone's door it would be two paratroopers, thirty-four year old Flight Sergeant Patrick Maloney from County Limerick and thirty-three year old Staff Sergeant Mervyn Evans from Capel Curig in Wales. In June 1959, dressed in their military fatigues and army boots, they marched 897 miles from John O'Groats to Land's End in eighteen days and seventeen hours. They were hailed as heroes by the *Daily Mail* who claimed they were the first men to walk End to End for more than a hundred years.

It was still rare in the 1950s for anyone to walk John O'Groats to Land's End. There were no national trails, long distance footpaths, or accepted route and the walk did not have the iconic status as a quintessentially British trek which it has today. Indeed, Maloney and Evans were instrumental in raising the profile of this walk although it is questionable if, as the *Daily Mail* claimed, they were the first to walk it for a hundred years.

Curiously, the first person recorded as walking End to End was not even British, but was American statesman Elihu Brurritt. Born in New Britain, Connecticut in 1810 Brurritt trained as a blacksmith, yet despite his humble origins he rose to be appointed by Abraham Lincoln as the United States Consul to Birmingham, England (not Birmingham, Alabama) in 1863. He acquired the nickname of the 'Learned Blacksmith' and had a long and illustrious diplomatic career in pursuit of temperance, world peace and the fight against slavery. He travelled widely and took the opportunity, while living in England to walk first from London to John O'Groats in 1863, then from London to Land's End and back the following year and he published accounts of both walks.

The first continuous End to End walk was most likely in 1871 by brothers Robert and John Naylor from Cheshire. The account of their walk, *From John O'Groats to Land's End*, was written by John Naylor but not published until 1916, forty-five years after their walk and after Robert had died. In 1879, a few years after the Naylor brothers and rather more in tune with some of Butlin's more eccentric walkers was

Robert Carlyle, a Cornishman who walked the entire way pushing his suitcase along in a wheelbarrow.

Sergeants Maloney and Evans followed their End to End trek with two more major walks in Britain. They marched from Edinburgh to Marble Arch in a record breaking six days, nine hours and fourteen minutes, averaging sixty miles a day. Then in March 1960 they topped even that by walking coast to coast across the 'waist of England,' maintaining a staggering pace of sixty-three miles a day.

If Maloney and Evans had unwittingly started a new trend for marathon walking it wasn't long before others began to follow. At first it was mostly servicemen tackling major treks, but soon civilians were joining in as well.

Lance corporal John Sinclair and Captain Stuart Heighton tramped 110 miles from Leicester to Charing Cross. Former paratrooper Joe Barraclough set out to walk 117 miles from Carlisle to Manchester, and Admiralty workers Roger Pascoe and David Painter left Bath to walk to London, wearing bowler hats and carrying rolled umbrellas. On the south coast, Tom Rowley, along with Walter Latham, took twenty-two hours and fifteen minutes to walk from Brighton to Charing Cross and back again, while in Plymouth a couple of naval men set out to walk 150 miles to Bristol.

These walks were unregulated and initially done just for fun, but it wasn't long before businesses, scenting a new craze and the commercial opportunities which went along with it, were offering sponsorship and cash prizes for anyone who broke walking records.

Land's End to John O'Groats was too big an undertaking for most marathon walkers. At the very least it required a fortnight away from work and some serious consideration as to logistics and planning. However, the 110 miles from Birmingham to Marble Arch, which could be walked in a weekend, quickly became a popular distance and competition for the record was fierce.

Sergeants Maloney & Evans in New York after their trek across the USA.

By late November 1959 marathon walking was in full swing and while the newspapers reported on the many recorded attempts, its newsworthiness was considered to be limited. Even the exploits of Maloney and Evans generated just a few column inches, and then only on the inside pages. For it to become a good story what the media needed was a figurehead, a celebrity, a human face for the new sensation in marathon walking. Ideally someone who was larger than life, an eccentric, a colourful human interest story. They found all of this and much, much more in the diminutive, yet very determined form of Dr Barbara Moore.

Russian by birth, Dr Moore looked at least ten years younger than her stated age of fifty-six. She claimed an impressive pedigree; a doctor of medicine, a qualified engineer, a pilot, a 'Heroine of the Soviet Union' and the all-Russia motorcycle champion. Yet it was none of these attributes which inspired her distance walking. She set out with the goal of using the new trend for mammoth walks as a vehicle to demonstrate her belief in the superiority of eating a very strict vegetarian diet of raw vegetables, fruit, nuts and honey, a diet she firmly believed would enable her to live for 150 years and to have a baby when she was 100.

Few could keep pace with her as she strode along on her treks dressed in a sheepskin coat, tracksuit, headscarf, plimsolls and motorcycle goggles. And to stave off any feelings of loneliness she might have during the long and weary hours on the road, packed in a shopping bag and tucked up with a hot water-bottle for warmth, she carried her pet baby tortoise. He was called Fangio.

8

Chapter Two: Doctor Babs

DR BARBARA MOORE ACHIEVED CELEBRITY in her native Russia in 1928 when, as the only female competitor amongst thirty men, she came second in a 5,000 mile motorcycle trial, racing from Moscow to Tiflis and back on her American built 'Indian' motorbike. She did not hit the headlines in the United Kingdom however until July 1959, some thirty-one years later when, aged fifty-six, she was disqualified from the *Daily Mail* Cross-Channel Blériot Race for arriving twenty minutes late at a check point.

In a strange quirk of fate, given the way events would unfold a mere seven months later, Billy Butlin was also a competitor, if a rather more successful one, in the same Blériot Race. Unlike the contests which made her famous in Russia, or the races which would quickly make her a household name in Britain, the Blériot was neither a motorcycle nor a walking race.

IN 1908, WHEN AVIATION WAS still a novelty and the preserve of daredevils and barnstormers, the *Daily Mail* offered a prize of £500 to anyone who could fly across the English Channel in a craft heavier than air. Balloons filled with hydrogen had already flown the Channel: an unmanned crossing in 1784; the following year Jean-Pierre Blanchard and John Jeffries made the first manned balloon flight across 'la Manche.'

In the same way as the Billy Butlin's John O'Groats to Land's End race fifty-two years later would be dismissed by some as a publicity stunt, many regarded the *Daily Mail's* 1908 challenge in the same light. With no takers at the first time of asking the *Mail* doubled the prize money the following year. This time a prize of £1,000 proved a strong inducement for French engineer Louis Blériot, a man who had made his fortune developing and manufacturing headlights for trucks. On 25th July 1909 he took off from Calais in his Type XI monoplane and flew at an altitude of 250 feet, at an approximate speed of forty-five miles per hour across the Channel, before making a heavy landing on a patch of sloping ground not far from Dover Castle.

Blériot's flight entered the history books, elevated him to the status of a celebrity, and served to demonstrate how air travel had the potential to be developed as a means of international travel. By 1959, commercial air travel was a firm reality, and the *Daily Mail* issued a second challenge: a Cross-Channel race from Marble Arch in London to the Arc de Triomphe in Paris. This was to commemorate the fiftieth anniversary of Blériot's flight and to highlight the need for improved transport links between the two national capitals.

The race, which took place over a ten day period between 13th and 23rd July 1959, generated a huge amount of public interest and produced a flood of entries, including many from celebrities of the day. Formula One racing driver Sterling Moss entered, as did Christine Blériot, cousin of Louis Blériot himself. Colette Duval, the glamourous model, actress and record breaking parachutist, boldly declared, 'For this race I am France.' Sadly she proved a more successful parachutist and actress than Cross-Channel racer when her pilot mistook a disused runway at Kenley airfield for Biggin Hill and they crashed through a fence.

Alongside the serious contenders were the eccentric and the downright whacky. They used every imaginable form of transport; limousines to roller skates, jet fighters to soapboxes and lawnmowers to push-bikes. Competitors hoping to post a fast time employed a combination of motorbikes and sports cars for land-based legs in both England and France. A quick dash from Marble Arch to a temporary heliport, of which there were at least three built along the River Thames, a helicopter to whisk them for the short hop to a private airfield where a fast plane would be on the runway ready for take-off, and then a high speed flight across the Channel.

Speed in the air wasn't the problem but congestion and traffic lights on the ground were. One solution was to have a second motorbike revved up and ready at the far side of traffic signals. If there was a lengthy delay, the racer could sprint across the road, dodging the traffic, and hop on the pillion of the second bike at the far side of the junction. Billy Butlin arranged for Donald Campbell, the land speed record breaker, to drive him from Marble Arch in a Porsche while his Redcoats held up traffic at road junctions. The police took a dim view of this however and put an end to it for his subsequent attempts.

Even on day one of competition, times of less than an hour between London to Paris were being posted. Captain 'Red Rory' Bamford Walker of the SAS set the early pace with a time of just fifty-seven minutes. The race was eventually won by thirty-five year old Squadron Leader Charles Maughan (later to become Air Vice-Marshal Maughan) in a time of forty minutes and forty-four seconds.

Billy Butlin bought a two seater World War II Spitfire especially for the race. It didn't have an engine but he managed to find one in Brussels and have engineers fit it into his plane. He made a temporary heliport at Chelsea Reach on the Thames by dumping several tons of gravel on the foreshore and arranged for a helicopter to fly him from there to the airfield at Biggin Hill where his Spitfire was waiting. Dressed in a set of dazzling white flying overalls with the letter 'B' proudly displayed on his breast pocket, he recorded the very respectable time of seventy minutes and twenty seconds coming third in his class. His winnings, a mere £100, didn't go very far towards covering his expenses which topped more than £5000.

Dr Moore's Blériot Race was a much less costly affair and rather more sedate, though not sedate enough. When she was racing from Marble Arch through Hyde Park the police clocked her bubble car doing forty-four miles per hour in a twenty zone and fined her two pounds.

If her attempt was a little too swift on the English leg of her race, she was far too slow on the other side of the Channel. She flew from Croydon to Le Touquet then ran to Beauvals. From there she had planned to ride a motorbike to St Denis and run the final leg to the Arc de Triomphe, but she arrived at a check point twenty minutes too late. When stewards disqualified her she burst into tears. The *Daily Mail* ran a feature on her a few days later under the by-line 'They Did it by Jet & Grass Juice'. They described her as the 'Most colourful character' in the race, 'the woman who jogged through France for nine hours accompanied by her pet tortoise'.

DESPITE THE DISTRACTIONS OF CROSS-Channel races, by November 1959 the marathon walking craze in Britain was at its height. A record time of thirty-four hours, forty minutes between Birmingham and Marble Arch had been set on the weekend of the 14th and 15th of November by two army sappers and suddenly the race was on to beat their time. Dr Moore, who was twice the age of most other walkers and had been living on a diet of just fruit, raw vegetables and nuts for more than twenty years, left Birmingham and covered the 110 miles to Marble Arch in a very creditable twenty-seven hours and thirty minutes. She took Fangio along with her again in a bag and from time to time would stop off at police stations along the way and ask them to boil a kettle so she could top-up Fangio's hot water bottle.

But not everyone accepted her time at face value. These walks, unlike organised athletic meetings where times were recorded officially, were unregulated and open to abuse. There were murmurings that she was faking these results. How could a woman of fifty-six, living on just fruit and salads, knock more than seven hours off the time set by fit servicemen? Dr Moore reacted angrily, declaring that she was not a faker and would prove it by repeating the walk the following weekend. And that's exactly what she did. This time, she covered the distance in twenty-six hours and twenty-nine minutes, cutting more than an hour off the time she'd set the previous weekend.

She set out from the Airport Hotel at Birmingham dressed in a purple tracksuit and plimsolls, accompanied this time by local marathon walker Philip Malins who followed her in his car with her supplies of honey and water. He was acting as an escort, support and, one suspects, as an unofficial verifier. Fangio the tortoise stayed at home.

Through vile weather she battled on making only two brief stops, eight minutes for a power-nap on Saturday night and a pause for just one minute thirteen miles out from Marble Arch.

Philip Malins, who was sceptical at the start had to quickly revise his opinion. 'I thought she was a phoney,' he told the *Daily Mirror*, 'but after this weekend I've changed my mind… She has incredible endurance.'

On the A5, early on Sunday morning, she slipped off the kerb and wrenched her thigh. Malins tied a handkerchief around it and she battled on. For the last few miles she was exhausted and seemed close to collapse as she trudged on through the rain, soaked to the skin with her head lolling from side to side. But at 12:14 pm she finally arrived at Marble Arch.

Sadly even this monumental effort wasn't enough to secure her the record. So competitive had this distance become that just the day before the record had been broken by three soldiers.

After this second Birmingham to Marble Arch walk, her commitment and endurance were no longer in question and it became clear to the media that *she*, rather than her endurance walks, was the story. The public love an eccentric, and if that eccentric is a plucky, colourful character with a hint of mystery thrown in, then so much the better. The *Daily Mirror* affectionately dubbed her 'Dr Babs' and her exploits would earn her several column inches of newsprint and a photograph, while the squaddies, who, on that occasion, were the real record breakers, had to suffer the ignominy of not even having their names printed.

YET THERE SEEMED TO BE a shadier side to Dr Moore. Whenever the press asked her why she was setting out on these marathon treks she would try to deflect them with arch statements such as 'I did it to prove I'm not a fraud', or 'to show that women have as much endurance as men.' She undoubtedly enjoyed her celebrity, or at least she enjoyed it to the point where the media began to probe into her personal life; then she could become evasive, mysterious and even downright hostile. On one occasion she threatened *Daily Mail* reporter Herbert Kretzmer with a 'Norfolk Slasher,' a particularly vicious hedging knife, when she decided his questions were becoming too intrusive.

It seemed clear, even at this early stage in her walking career, that she had no real interest in the marathon walks themselves. For her they were a vehicle to highlight her radical views about diet, health and longevity. She was a committed and radical vegetarian at a time when vegetarianism was by no means common in Britain. Over the years she had experimented with almost every type of vegetarian diet. She had lived on chickweed from Clapham Common or grass from Kensington Gardens until she finally settled on a diet of fruit, nuts, raw vegetables and honey, a regime which most dietitians would agree was healthy, if a little unexciting. On this diet she seemed healthy and to have the energy to make her record breaking walks. Indeed most people who met her commented on her excellent complexion and how she looked a couple of decades younger than her fifty-six years.

Undoubtedly having trained as a medical doctor gave weight to her theories and soon members of the public were beginning to take an interest in her dietary regime. When questioned a little more closely, however, Dr Moore's medical credentials began to appear a little suspect and her dietary theories became more extreme, to the point of quackery. She believed that, given the right kind of nourishment and practicing abstinence from alcohol, sex and harmful foods (she considered protein to be a 'horrible poison'), a person was capable of living indefinitely. Despite being married three times, she and her husband art teacher and sculptor Harry Moore (not to be confused with the more famous sculptor Henry Moore) practiced celibacy. She confidently expected to live to somewhere between 150 to 200 years and she planned to have a baby when she was 100. Even the most courageous interviewer baulked at challenging her on how she could expect to conceive at 100 years old if she was celibate. But there was yet more: her dietary ideas extended to the point of her being a 'Breatharian', a person who does not eat but lives on sunlight and fresh air.

'When I go to Switzerland,' she told *Daily Mail* reporter Shirley Flack, 'I shall live for three to four months on nothing but water and fresh air. I believe that where the air is fresh and unpolluted food is not necessary.'

THE INK WAS BARELY DRY on the newsprint before Dr Moore was off again. Less than three weeks after her success walking Birmingham to Marble Arch she set out on 18th December, this time on a much longer walk: 373 miles from Edinburgh to London, which she planned to complete in seven days.

Wherever Barbara Moore was concerned drama and controversy were never far behind. Before she had even left London she was knocked off her husband's motorbike on the way to Victoria Coach Station. Uninjured she left Harry to sort out the mess while she flagged down a passing motorist and got him to drive her to the rest of the way so she was able to catch her coach to Edinburgh.

There was something of a spat in the Scottish capital when she publicly called the Lord Provost of Edinburgh 'ungallant' after he had refused to give her a message to deliver to the Queen. She said she had been planning to stop by at Buckingham Palace when she reached London to give her good wishes to Her Majesty.

At more than three times the distance of her Birmingham to Marble Arch treks, this walk was to prove to be an altogether tougher undertaking. The marathon walking craze had started during the balmy days of summer. The Scottish borders in late December were another matter entirely and she was forced to battle her way through severe headwinds and rain. She had another road accident in Northumberland when a car knocked her into a ditch. Again she was unhurt but badly shaken and needed to rest for two hours before she felt fit to continue.

Two days before Christmas the *Daily Mail* reported 'Dr Barbara Denies 14-Mile Lift'. This was one of the first indications of the cheating and rumour mongering which would later come to bedevil the marathon walking craze. Yet it was clear from the many people, not least the press, who were following her progress closely, that she did not take lifts. She may have been quirky, she may have been eccentric, she was undoubtedly difficult and had extreme views about diet and health, but she was no fraud. There was never any evidence of her cheating in either her motorcycle races in Russia or her marathon walking exploits in Britain. If anything, the reverse was true. She drove herself on beyond the point of exhaustion: even when her feet were sore, swollen and blistered and she really should have stopped to give them the chance to recover.

By this time she had become a favourite of the public. Lorry drivers hooted as they drove past, well-wishers shook her by the hand and gave her gifts of fruit and honey. At one point she had a procession of 150 cars following her along the Great North Road. She joked that she was determined to reach London in time to do her Christmas shopping.

Her exploits and ideas on diet had so engaged the public that people who had never considered marathon walking before were soon setting out on their own treks to emulate her. Robert Race and Robert Hutchinson, two pupils from St Paul's School set out to walk through the night from London to Oxford, a distance of about fifty-five miles. They left Hammersmith just after nine one evening and had covered somewhere in the region of thirty-five miles and reached Stokenchurch when the rain set in. They took cover in a bus shelter where they promptly fell asleep. The next thing they knew they were being shaken awake by a policeman demanding to know who they were and what they were up to. They explained about Dr Moore and how they were walking to Oxford. As it was still lashing down with rain the policeman packed them into the back seat of his patrol car and gave them a lift for the rest of the way to Oxford where they arrived just in time for breakfast.

In January 1960 the police were again called in to track down a youngster setting out to copy Dr Moore. This time it was a nine year old lad, described as 'the Trolley Boy'. He had become obsessed with Dr Moore's marathon walking and had secretly slipped away from home. He was thought to be walking somewhere along the A1 following Dr Bab's example.

St Paul's schoolboys Roberts Race and Hutchinson were not finished with their Dr Moore adventures quite yet, either. After failing to reach Oxford in the autumn they set out the following February to walk what had become the classic 110 mile marathon walker's trek from London to Robert Hutchinson's home in Birmingham. They set out again from Hammersmith and covered forty miles through the night reaching Wendover in the small hours. Here, once more, the call of breakfast proved stronger than that of the road. They dropped in on another friend for breakfast and he drove them the rest of the way to Birmingham. As Robert Hutchinson said in 2016, 'Barbara Moore would no doubt have thought us a couple of wimps for only managing thirty-five to forty miles on each occasion.'

Dr Barbara Moore. Note her feet wrapped in sackcloth.

By the time Dr Moore had reached Bedfordshire, on her Edinburgh to London trek, the constant pounding her feet were taking from tarmacked roads had reduced them to a terrible state. In the late 1950s and early 1960s sports footwear was pretty basic. There were no Nike or Adidas springy air-cushioned running shoes or trainers back then. For marathon walkers or runners there were just rubber-soled plimsolls or baseball boots and not very much as an alternative.

Despite managing to sleep for five hours at Biggleswade she had something of a crisis of confidence on Christmas Eve forty-five miles out from the capital. She had abandoned her famous plimsolls by this time. The only footwear she could tolerate on her swollen and blistered feet were fur boots which she'd wrapped in sackcloth and rubber and tied in place with string. Her usual brisk pace along the road was slowed to a painful two miles per hour.

She set out on these walks with no formal support team and had to rely on help from strangers, well-wishers and the reporters who were covering her progress for the press. One such reporter was the *Daily Mail's* Michael Borissow. He would let her take rests in his car and carry fruit juice and spare socks for her in the boot. For the first time since setting out she was on the point of giving up, but he had a message to pass on from her husband Harry to say that he was on his way to meet her. This news seemed to revitalise her, to restore her sense of purpose, and she was quickly back on the road again and walking steadily, if gingerly and painfully, in the direction of London.

Sadly, despite Michael Borissow's help, and that of other members of the press pack, her relationship with the news media, and the *Daily Mail* in particular, was set to sour within just a few months.

As events transpired, far from calling at Buckingham Palace to offer the Queen her good wishes, the only place Dr Moore was fit to go when she finally reached London was Ward Three at Paddington General Hospital, where she needed emergency treatment for her badly blistered and bruised feet.

ON THE 22ND OF NOVEMBER 1959 the Sunday newspaper *The News of the World* announced its 'March of the Century', a rather grand title for a walk following the now very well-trodden route between Birmingham and London. The race, exclusively for members of the armed forces, was intended to play to patriotic sentiments and boost the profile of the military. There was a trophy for the winners and a £1,000 prize to be donated to a Services charity.

The announcement met with a favourable response from assorted top brass in the military, with a War Office spokesman calling it, 'An excellent idea.' The race itself took place on the weekend of 18th December 1959 with 228 walkers setting off in pairs at one minute intervals.

Far from being the 'March of the Century', it would have been better titled the 'Limp of the Century' or even the 'Wimp of the Century'. *The News of the World* tried to put a brave public face on an event which did little to showcase the fitness or the endurance of the armed forces. The weather was appalling. Racers marched in pairs, released in one-minute intervals, which resulted in competitors dashing off to catch the pair ahead of them and consequently burning themselves out, rather than conserving their energy. Everyone had to wear regulation army boots, so blisters quickly became a problem and most competitors dropped out long before the end. With only a handful of confirmed finishers the paper hid the results away on page three and there were no photos. The only photograph accompanying the article was one of Dr Moore recovering in hospital and showing off her bandaged feet.

AS DR MOORE WAS DISCHARGED from hospital on the 28th December, *The Times* were reporting that Wilfred McDougall, a garage owner from Staffordshire, had put up a prize of £250 to anyone who could beat her Edinburgh to London time. The first to take up the challenge was James Holdsworth, a joiner from Bradford. He fared even less well than the lads from St Paul's School abandoning his attempt after just twenty-seven miles.

On the 5th January 1960 the *Times* reported that Mr Terry Haywood, a lorry driver from Birmingham, had taken more than a day off Dr Barbara Moore's time and had claimed the prize of £250. Dr Moore didn't hesitate to respond. The following day she announced her intention to walk 1,000 miles from John O'Groats to Land's End and said she would start next week. She invited Mr Haywood to join her. He said, 'No.'

Chapter Three: The Woman from Soviet Russia

FOR ALL OF HER HIGH profile marathon walks, celebrity and media interviews, Dr Barbara Moore herself remained something of an enigma, her past deliberately cloaked in mystery.

She spoke with a strong accent yet when *Daily Mail* reporter Olga Franklin attempted to speak to her in Russian she seemed totally bewildered. Neither could she or her husband understand a letter she had received, apparently from the Russian Embassy. She said she was a qualified doctor yet all accounts of her practicing were vague and unsubstantiated, and some of her claims about nutrition and the human body suggested a somewhat eccentric perception of the most basic aspects of anatomy and physiology. In addition she purported to be an engineer, a pilot, a motorbike champion, an expert on diet and now, a record breaking marathon walker. She was supposed to have been diagnosed with leukaemia in 1954 by a specialist from Harley Street and given just five months to live. Since then she had recovered while the Harley Street specialist had died. Then there were her extravagant claims about needing no nutrition other than fresh air and water, her plans of living to 150 and giving birth to a baby when she reached 100.

When pressed too hard by reporters she would become obstructive and abrasive, as Herbert Kretzmer could attest to after his interview with the Dr Moore and the 'Norfolk Slasher'.

Hoping for a more sympathetic hearing, reporters tried approaching her husband. Harry Moore, five years younger than his wife, was a friendly and kind natured man, with dark hair, sideburns and the looks of a matinee-idol gone a little to seed. They had married in Fulham in 1939 just a few weeks before the start of World War II, when he was twenty-seven and she was thirty-two. In most news reports at the time of her marathon walks he is described as a sculptor yet it is apparent from official documents that he mostly worked as an art teacher and later as an art director in films. Despite a marriage of twenty years by 1959, he seemed cowed and overawed in Barbara's presence. He was 'like a shy schoolboy summoned before the Head to explain some misdemeanour,' said Herbert Kretzmer; when Olga Franklin wanted to ask her about the message from the Russian Embassy Harry Moore urged caution. 'Depends how you ask her,' he said. The only information he would part with was that her mother had been a German countess. He wouldn't even tell Franklin Dr Barbara's maiden name, as 'she might not like it.' And he claimed to have forgotten her previous married name.

Dr Moore was a remarkable individual who led a remarkable life. She succeeded in reinventing herself several times over and was not averse to modifying her past in order to enhance or romanticise her public image. She published two autobiographies, the first in 1943 under the title *I am a Woman from Soviet Russia*, when it went almost unnoticed in the closing months of World War II. The second was serialised in *The People* in 1960 just a few days after her triumphant walk from John O'Groats to Land's End at the pinnacle of her popularity and fame. In these accounts and many of her interviews with the press she seemed to deliberately cultivate an air of mystery, refusing to cite her family name or the names of key players in her life, hiding them behind shadowy anonyms such as 'Mr A' (her second husband) or 'Commander Z' (a senior figure in the Russian military she had a falling out with in 1933).

DR BARBARA MOORE WAS BORN Anya Nikolaievna Cherkasova on 22nd of December 1905 near Stalingrad in Russia and spent most of her early life at Saratov on the banks of the Volga River.

She cited two differing accounts of her family and early life. Shortly after her End to End walk, she was claiming to come from an affluent and noble family with a large estate just south of Stalingrad. Her mother, said Dr Barbara, was a 'Russian aristocrat – very high born – of the old school.' The family was wealthy and held huge shooting parties. It was at one of these parties that she claimed to have been bitten by a rabid dog and had to be rushed by train to the Pasteur Institute in Paris. Her family were robbed of their estates during the revolution and reviled as bourgeois.

Her earlier account, from 1943, was probably more accurate. Anya, along with her two younger sisters, came from a moderately well-off family. Her father Vasilii Egorovich Cherkasova, a kind-hearted and generous man, was a lawyer who had inherited some land and an estate along with his brothers. Her mother was not a German countess, as third husband Harry had reported, and it is questionable if she was the high-born Russian aristocrat as Dr Barbara later claimed. What is apparent is that her mother, in contrast with her father, was strong-willed and severe; characteristics which the young Anya had clearly inherited.

This comfortable early life was disrupted in 1914 by the outbreak of the First World War when her father, despite his age, was recalled to the army, then disrupted again in 1917 by the Russian Revolution. Despite their relatively wealthy background her father sided with the revolutionaries and was part of the Volynsky Regiment which stormed the Winter Palace in Petrograd to demand the Tsar step down. Probably due to her father's influence and her being at school through this period of turbulence where the curriculum reflected the new political standpoint, she readily adopted the views of the new Soviet regime and broadly maintained that viewpoint throughout her life. Indeed she dedicated her first book, *I am a Woman from Soviet Russia*, to 'THE GREAT RUSSIAN PEOPLE' and 'THE SOVIET LEADERS – WHO LED THOSE PEOPLE TO THE HEIGHTS.' The only time she seemed to baulk at the Russian political system was when its restrictions, regulations or the law got in the way of the things she wanted to do. When this was the case she had no qualms whatsoever about pursuing her own desires and became indignant whenever this brought her into conflict with the authorities.

An early indication of her disdain for rules and regulations came in 1919 when she falsified her age to get into university a year early (at fifteen and a half instead of sixteen and a half). She later claimed to have bribed the Registrar of Births to change her age on her birth certificate. She studied medicine at Saratov University where one of her duties as a student was to collect corpses from the hospital mortuary and take them on a horse drawn sledge back to the university for dissection. While this was a grizzly task for the young Anya, all went well until the occasion when one of the 'corpses' woke up. The man had been dead drunk rather than actually dead and his body was so frozen by the winter weather that the presiding doctor had mistaken it for rigor mortis.

The life of a student in post-revolutionary Russia was very hard. They studied in unheated buildings and were only allowed such meagre rations that there was a very real danger of starving to death. In 1922 a commission for the relief of the Russian famine, headed by the arctic explorer and humanitarian Dr Fridjof Nansen, visited Saratov University to provide additional rations for the students. Anya Cherkasova had by this time established herself as a prominent and active student. She was president of the students' Philosophico-Religious Society and had been elected as the representative from the Medical Faculty on the committee overseeing the distribution of these rations. The students would get one hot meal a day of butter beans, white bread and cocoa and part of Anya's job was to oversee this food being delivered from the storerooms to the kitchens. Other students may have found this something of a bland diet but young Anya didn't mind the absence of meat because she had decided, much to her mother's disgust, to become a vegetarian when she was just fourteen.

With the benefit of hindsight she would have been wiser to keep a low profile and just concentrate on her studies. The aftermath of any revolution is an unstable time when suspicion is rife and there is the ever present fear of counter revolution. These committees, particularly Nansen's famine relief committee, brought Anya into contact with foreigners who, the authorities thought, might well be involved in spying. Anya was arrested by the GPU (the State Political Directorate or secret police and forerunner of the KGB) and put in a cell. This would prove to be the first of her many arrests and episodes in custody. She was held for a week on suspicion of being in contact with foreigners before being fingerprinted and released on a sort of probation where she was allowed to resume her studies at the university while the matter was investigated further. She had to 'sign on' at the GPU each day and was forbidden to move outside a three mile limit. She later discovered that a member of the Nansen committee, an Englishman, had been secretly writing to her. These letters, which she claimed to be totally ignorant of, had been intercepted by the GPU. Nonetheless contact with outsiders reflected badly on her. She had been denounced by two of her student associates and despite protesting her innocence she received the word from a friendly GPU officer that she was to be exiled to the Solovetsky Islands in the far north which would put an end to her studies and any hope of becoming a doctor. She was determined this would not happen. By this point Anya had completed five years of study and was able to graduate as a general practitioner. However, the threat of exile to the Solovetsky Islands prevented her progressing to train for her chosen specialism surgery.

SUICIDES AMONGST STUDENTS WERE COMMON in this post-revolutionary period, so Anya decided to fake her own death, escape to Moscow, and there throw herself on the mercy of the Nansen Committee. She stuffed her doctor's diploma, university papers and passport into the pockets of her overcoat and arranged for a friend to leave it strategically by a hole in the ice on the frozen Volga River. The authorities, she hoped, would then assume she had taken her own life. While this attempt to fake her own death may have fooled the authorities into writing it off as just another student suicide, it left her with a problem. She would need a 'passport' to travel by train to Moscow. The 'passport' was really personal identity papers rather than a document for overseas travel. Russian citizens were not allowed to travel abroad at this time, as she would discover later to her cost.

So Anya Cherkasova the medical student became Barbara Beliaeva the qualified doctor. She stole a friend's passport and left the name Anya Cherkasova behind forever. She would later claim that she and Barbara Beliaeva had agreed to exchange passports; however her 1943 account contradicts this. She states how she chose her moment when she was able to get hold of Barbara's handbag to steal the passport and admits she was 'aware [she] was committing a crime' yet felt she had to do it. That she was desperate and fearful of exile to the Solovetsky Islands must go some way to mitigate her crime, yet it remained a mean trick to pull on a friend. It would have been especially traumatic for Barbara Beliaeva as she had only just had her passport replaced after she lost her original one.

ANYA CHERKASOVA, NOW BARBARA BELIAEVA, arrived in Moscow and asked for help from Nansen's organisation and the American Relief Administration (ARA) which no doubt placed them in something of a dilemma. They were foreign aid organisations, Non-governmental Organisations or NGOs as they would be termed today. Assisting a fugitive, particularly one who was a criminal, which she now was, could jeopardise their whole operation in Russia, not to mention the potential political or diplomatic fallout. Yet how could they turn her over to the authorities? The officer into whose lap this particular problem landed was Count Serge Tolstoi, the grandson of Leo Tolstoi, the celebrated Russian writer. He decided to deal with this matter in the time-honoured fashion of dumping it on somebody else's plate, preferably somebody as far away from Moscow as possible. So he bought her a railway ticket and shipped her off to the ARA offices in Leningrad.

Count Tolstoi had given Barbara a letter of introduction to his counterpart in Leningrad who, in keeping with the Russian literary theme, was Mikhail Chekhov, the playwright's nephew. Leningrad it seemed didn't want this runaway on their hands any more than Moscow did, so they arranged for Barbara to join two students from Leningrad University, sons of wealthy businessmen living in Germany, who were planning to escape secretly abroad. She did indeed join them on their clandestine escape but when she landed in Finland she lost her nerve, changed her mind, decided she couldn't leave her homeland and paid the boatman to take her back to Russia again.

It's not hard to imagine how frustrated Mikhail Chekhov must have felt when this difficult young woman arrived back in Leningrad after his best efforts, and not inconsiderable expense, to get her out of the country and beyond the reach of the GPU. He couldn't do much more than tell her she would just have to lie low and wait until something turned up.

It was during the time Barbara was kicking her heels in Leningrad, waiting for 'something to turn up' that she first started to experiment with diet and fasting. She went along with her landlady to the religious gatherings of a charismatic preacher Father Anisimus who encouraged his followers to abstain from food and water for periods of up to five days in order to 'mortify one's flesh' and become nearer to God. He also encouraged them to part with their valuables and donate them to his church, but as Barbara had neither money nor valuables this particular aspect of his ministry didn't trouble her. Throughout her life Barbara seemed to constantly be searching for a cause to which she could commit her considerable strength of will, and she embraced the idea of denying herself food and water with enthusiasm.

She began fasting for one day at a time but this was not enough for her and she quickly increased this to week-long fasts. She believed that when a person accepts an idea or concept they should embrace it totally. 'I respect a person who is definite,' she said, '… and proves it … I scorn those who compromise in life on a little of this with a little of that.' This outlook would shape her whole life and underpin her substantial achievements in her studies, her competitive motorcycle racing, her approach to diet, and eventually her marathon walks. It would also prove to be self-defeating, especially in regard to her responsibilities to the people around her, her casual lack of concern for the safety of others and her attitude to any form of authority which attempted to stand in her way.

How much Dr Barbara internalised her medical training must be open for question at this point, especially with regard to her cavalier approach to fasting. Not eating for seven days may be acceptable on spiritual grounds, but not drinking is extremely hazardous, yet the medically trained Barbara seemed to have been blissfully unaware of the dangers of dehydration. When she later went seven days without eating and drinking during a very warm spring in Tiflis, she seemed surprised that her skin became cracked, her eyes dry and her lips parched.

Barbara quickly became disenchanted with the charlatan Father Anisimus and stopped attending his meetings. Her position in Leningrad was still perilous, all the more so after a chance meeting with an acquaintance from Saratov who hailed her as Anya Cherkasova and said he had never truly believed that she had committed suicide under the ice of the Volga River. After this encounter she decided she needed to leave Leningrad as a matter of urgency. Her friends clubbed together to buy her a railway ticket and in what she described as a 'semi-disguised manner' they sent her out to the Ukraine on the fastest train available.

She was armed with a letter of introduction to a Dr Djigoorda at the hospital in Volchansk where she was only able to work as a volunteer because of the problems with her paperwork and assumed name. She did however manage to earn a little money to live on by coaching private pupils for their exams.

From Volchansk she moved to Tiflis in Georgia at the urging of a young engineer, Alexander Pataleev. But even here she was not free from her past and once again encountered one of her old enemies from Saratov. She was beginning to despair of her life as a fugitive and lived in constant fear of being denounced to the GPU, a knock on the door late at night, arrest and imprisonment. It was Alexander Pataleev who came up with the solution to her problem. He would marry her.

THROUGHOUT DR BARBARA MOORE'S EVENTFUL history, romance, love and, perish the thought, sex, are noticeable by their absence. She was an intelligent, wilful young person, slightly built with tidy features and long flowing blonde hair. It seems impossible that some of the young male students she studied with at Saratov University didn't feel attracted to her. If they did, she does not appear to have noticed. There was Mr K, a 'very handsome, athletic looking Czechoslovak officer' tasked by the ARA of seeing her onto the train from Moscow to Leningrad, who passionately kissed her when he saw her off and gave her a parcel containing chocolate with notepaper and envelopes so she could write to him. She never wrote. He even sent her a message via Count Tolstoi asking why she had never written. 'The handsome face of that dashing Czechoslovakian officer flashed into my memory,' she wrote much later, 'and I wished I could be less reticent!' Her next suiter must have been every bit as reticent as she, a young and very shy doctor from the hospital where she was working at in Volchansk. He only plucked up the courage to write and tell her how much he loved her when she was leaving.

Dr Moore married three times, had no children, and was always keen to point out the sexless nature of these marriages of convenience, backed up by her third husband Harry Moore in 1959. 'We don't live like a normal couple,' he told *Daily Mail* reporter Olga Franklin. '... We are both like grown-up children ... ours is a platonic marriage because we believe that sex also causes ageing of the body.'

Yet of all of her husbands, it was Alexander Pataleev to whom she was devoted. By Dr Barbara's standards husbands two and three paled by comparison. 'He was a big man,' she said, 'in every way ... tall, had enormous eyes and a very clean, clear complexion.' He neither smoked nor drank and was not, or so she said, interested in the physical side of a relationship or of having children.

He set out the terms of their marriage like a business contract. They would remain friends and she would have all the advantages of being married to him, a respected engineer. He earned enough money to be able to keep them both, they would live together in the same flat but each have their own room. They would be free to live their own lives, to have their own friends and, most importantly, Barbara Beliaeva would become Barbara Pataleev and be able to leave her past behind. If, at a later date either wanted to escape this arrangement to 'marry in earnest' they would be free to obtain a divorce. She celebrated her wedding by fasting for seven days.

Chapter Four: Road Rage

IT IS OPEN TO QUESTION if Dr Barbara's marriages were quite as platonic as she represented them, at least from the point of view of two of her three husbands. She was almost certainly projecting her own views onto the 'woman-hater', Alexander Pataleev. Here was the man who first coaxed her to move to Tiflis, who filled her room with fruit and flowers for her arrival, bought her the motorbikes she wanted and met her with armfuls of roses when work had kept them apart for some months.

Dr Barbara worked as her husband's assistant on his engineering projects in the remote and mountainous parts of Georgia. He built major state-sponsored projects such as bridges, tunnels and hydro-electric schemes. She acted as his secretary and also as medic to his team of engineers. Living in those remote regions she found the most practical way to get around was on horseback. She quickly taught herself to ride and (naturally) became an expert horsewoman. She developed a strong bond with her fiery Cossack horse Orel, who was as wilful and headstrong as she. On Orel's back she would ride like the wind and it was during these gallops that she discovered her new passion; speed.

In 1927 she abandoned any plans she may still have had for a career in medicine and, no doubt influenced by Alexander Pataleev's work, enrolled to study engineering at the Institute in Tiflis. Soon she was no longer satisfied with the speed of her horse, and in keeping with her new interest in engineering she developed a passion for motorcycles. There were no motorbikes being made in Russia at that time and they were a rare sight on Russian roads. Alexander arranged to have a 1,200 cc 'Indian' motorcycle imported from America for her. She always referred to it as her 'Red' Indian, and on this machine she would spend her every spare moment speeding along the Georgian Military Highway.

The following year she was invited to be one of the riders in a 5,000 mile motorbike trial-race from Moscow to Tiflis and back. Of the thirty riders taking part she was the only woman and for all of her protestations of being sexless, she clearly enjoyed being the sole woman in what was otherwise a man's world. The riders were supported by three trucks which followed them with spare parts, fuel and a team of medics. The whole enterprise was a government sponsored trial to see how well motorcycles coped with the road conditions in Russia with a view to assessing their military use in the future.

She rode her trusty 'Indian' which performed magnificently. The road conditions, especially in the rural areas were challenging. Most roads were unsurfaced and deeply rutted. In summer they were hard and dusty; after heavy rain they turned into rivers of mud. Mechanical breakdowns and punctures were a daily occurrence. They would spend their days riding and their evenings knocking their bikes back into shape after the battering they had taken on the Russian roads. Most of the traffic in the rural areas were farm-carts pulled by horses who had frequently cast shoes leaving nails scattered on the road or imbedded in the mud. Soon the Indian's tyres consisted of more patches than inner tube.

Dr Barbara was awarded second place overall and, as the only woman, became, for the first time in her life, the darling of the Russian media. There was extensive local and national newspaper coverage with photos of her being embraced by senior party officials displayed in shop windows across Moscow.

She clearly loved her new media profile and all the fuss which went along with it. She was invited to government events, attended dinners, was awarded gold badges and presented with special certificates to commemorate her achievement. The only downside to her new fame was that she was still a fugitive from the law. She may have changed her name and reinvented herself, but she was still the woman who had faked her own death and stolen a friend's identity. Being in the public eye did not sit well with her history and it was inevitable that sooner or later the past would catch up with her. This time instead of running she decided to meet the problems head on. After all she was no longer just a penniless medical student from Saratov, she was married to a senior state engineer, a national sports star in her own right and one who had powerful friends in the Communist Party. She made a clean breast of the problems of her past to the authorities who initiated an investigation and, after a suitable period for deliberation, decided she had played no part in the alleged spying activities by members of Dr Nansen's American Relief Administration. On the matter of the stolen identity, it was decided that rather than trying to unravel the bureaucratic nightmare of which name belonged to who they decided to leave well alone. She was allowed to keep her current name of Barbara Pataleev and was freed with no penalty.

It was no doubt a shrewd move on the part of the authorities to let her keep her existing name, but not shrewd enough, for Dr Barbara's name or names became an integral part of the mystery which was her past. There is little doubt that her birth name was Anya Nikolaievna Cherkasova, yet when she married Harry Moore in 1939, she cited her name on the marriage certificate as Anya Nikolaievna PETIGURA late PATALEEFF formerly BELIAEFF. She also cited her father's name as Beliaeff when it clearly had been Cherkasova. It may be because of the ruling by authorities in 1929 that she stuck to a version of Beliaeva, the name she had stolen. She was also flexible about her use of her first husband's name. Mostly she referred to him rather formally as Mr Pataleev, but used Pataleewa for both his father and the hyphenated version of her name. Her maiden name, as recorded on her death certificate in 1977, is also cited incorrectly as Pataleewa.

IT'S HARD NOT TO FEEL a little sympathy for her husband, big hearted Alexander Pataleev. Dr Barbara clearly held him in great regard, if not affection, all of her life. He was the man who had married a 'wanted' woman in order to make her legal. They lived quite separate, and apparently platonic lives. Whether he was as happy with the sexless nature of their relationship as she was is less clear. It's not unreasonable to speculate that he agreed to, even suggested, these platonic arrangements to get this extraordinary woman to agree to marry him, hoping perhaps, in time, with a degree of mutual attraction and his undoubted kindness towards her, their relationship would develop into something more like a normal marriage. As it was they spent huge amounts of time apart. He was usually away supervising some major state engineering project somewhere out in the backwoods while she would be somewhere else in the country either involved in an engineering project herself or on one of her mammoth motorcycle rides.

Their relationship may best be summed up by the ring he bought her. It had the head of a golden lion biting onto a diamond. Pataleev said he wanted her to have it because all of her life she had been biting on something hard.

Dr Barbara celebrated her acquittal by rushing home, hastily reassembling her motorbike and going for a high speed ride. As she roared down the hill into town she left it until the last possible moment to slow down. When she applied the rear brake, nothing happened. She squeezed the front brake, again nothing. Both brakes had simultaneously failed. This was serious. Unable to stop she weaved her way through the traffic, narrowly missing a tram and almost colliding with a bus. The terrified passengers stared from the windows as she sped past. Car and lorry drivers blared their horns and swerved to get out of her way. When she was able to point the bike up a steep hill she finally managed to bring her machine under control and to come to a halt. The police were on the scene in an instant. They decided that anyone riding so wildly must be drunk. Inebriated or not she was clearly a danger to other road users, so they arrested her, impounded her motorbike and marched her off to the cells. She spent a night in custody until Alexander was able to get there the next morning and arrange for her release. When she got back home she found the Indian's brake linings had dried out and were no longer effective: something she had neglected to check in her rush to get out on the road for a high speed ride.

It seemed that from Dr Barbara's point of view her husband Alexander Pataleev served two main functions. Firstly he was able to provide her with the necessary funds and motorbikes for her to live her new life to the full and secondly, to always turn up at the right moment to get her out of jail.

MOST OF THE RUSSIAN MOTORCYCLE races Dr Barbara took part in were not held on racetracks but on public roads where there was still regular traffic and pedestrians to contend with. In those early days, motorbike races were more like rallies or time trials. For one such trial-race, they rode out to Iran, Persia as it was then, and returned via Armenia and

Turkey. She was racing with the rest of the pack, going flat-out along the final stretch of road into Tiflis when, there being no ropes or barriers to hold the crowd back, she narrowly missed two children who ran across the road in front of her. Again she was arrested, detained and put in a cell.

The crowd became incensed and mob violence was only narrowly avoided. The volatile atmosphere which followed resembled something between a French farce and a Greek tragedy. There were weeping parents, surly doctors and an angry, restive crowd. She was accused of killing the children who had been taken away to hospital by that time. Indeed the officiating doctor announced that they were dead. They were not. They were unharmed but badly shaken. Once more it required the intervention of Alexander, along with a delegation of motorcyclists and five days of negotiation to extract her from this situation.

IN 1931 SHE WAS ON the winning team in a 400 mile race for cars and motorbikes from Moscow to Gorky, after which she was allowed to import a new bike, a 1,200 cc Harley-Davidson, from the USA. With this new machine she set out to make a solo ride across Russia, 2,640 miles from Leningrad to Tiflis, a massive undertaking. Quite apart from the distance and the dreadful state of the country roads, this time she was making the ride without support. There would be no trucks following her with drums of fuel, mechanics and spare parts. Everything she needed had to be strapped onto the Harley or stowed in a sidecar (which she eventually ditched at Kharkov when its springs broke). It was an epic and heroic venture where she had to cope with appalling weather, mechanical breakdowns, the usual punctures and hair-raising river crossings. She was helped along the way by villagers, other motorbike enthusiasts and workers from the collective farms. Sometimes the benefit of this help was questionable. Arriving late one evening at a collective farm with the Harley almost unrecognisable from the amount of mud caked on it, the farm lads offered to clean her bike. They used high pressure hoses to wash the mud off then rags to polish the machine until it shone. Barbara was delighted. Or she was until next morning when the Harley refused to start. The hoses the boys had used flooded the carburettor with water and she had to strip it down and dry everything out before she could get on her way again.

Despite the Harley being a robust machine which performed magnificently on dreadful roads, she still suffered numerous breakdowns, and all of her engineering knowledge, skill and ingenuity came into play to make temporary repairs. Often she had to scavenge parts as and where she could. On one occasion she persuaded a local GPU officer to part with the front springs from his own Harley-Davidson so she could continue with her ride.

Finally she made it and was escorted for the last twenty miles into Tiflis by a column of motorcyclists. Once again she was the toast of Russia, in motorcycling circles at least, and the government made her 'The Champion Motor-cyclist of Russia.' Not only was this a great personal achievement, it also enhanced the profile of Soviet women. She became a role model for Russian women at a time when the government was trying to promote the idea of women driving tractors and lorries in the workplace and on communal farms. The government declared her 'Soviet Woman's Day Heroine'.

Fame opened opportunities to Dr Barbara that were denied the average Soviet citizen. She was a qualified engineer and in addition to taking part in adventurous motoring trials, she was also able to learn to pilot a glider, then a plane, and then to learn parachuting. She moved back to Leningrad followed by a somewhat reluctant Alexander Pataleev after he had finished his work in the Caucasus. He kept his own council about his wife's passion for speed, motorbikes and now flying. They were not the kind of things he was interested in. This may have been an early indication of cracks beginning to appear in their relationship.

A downside of her celebrity was that Dr Barbara became rather full of herself and her new superstar status, to the extent where she seemed to believe that she had more right to the highway than others and that matters of safety, particularly the safety of others, should come second to her love of speed. She may have become the Russian champion on a motorbike, but she quickly became a menace on the roads, especially in remote and agricultural areas, where horse-drawn carts or the odd slow moving tractor were more common. She collided with cows, pigs, chickens and ducks, all of whom came off the worst from their encounter with Dr Barbara and her Harley. There was the distressing incident with the two children on the road just outside Tiflis, and then in Leningrad in 1932 on a wet road she skittled over an eight-four year old lady who suffered a broken leg. The local traffic police were in despair. Inevitably there came a point when she overstepped the mark.

She was riding through the Square of Revolution in Leningrad one evening with 'Mr A', a young Englishman visiting Russia, on the pillion when she narrowly missed a married couple who were trying to cross the road. Angry words were exchanged and what started out as a road rage incident quickly escalated. The man grabbed hold of the bike's handlebars to stop her getting away. Dr Barbara slapped him across the face and then, ignoring his angry protests, she rode off.

Unbeknown to Dr Barbara and her pillion passenger, the man whose face she'd slapped was General Uritzky, the officer in charge of military operations for the whole of northern Russia and not a man to let such an insult pass. Dr Barbara was arrested and her Harley-Davidson impounded.

The charges were serious. The traffic police were keen to bring to heel this woman who seemed to think her celebrity as a Soviet Heroine gave her carte blanche to flaunt the laws of the road. They quickly formed an alliance with General Uritzky to build a case against her. Once again it fell to Alexander Pataleev to get Dr Barbara out of trouble. She was released later that evening but it became clear that the matter was serious and could drag on for some time.

THERE WERE FURTHER INDICATIONS AT this point that all may not have been well within their marriage. The passenger on her motorbike that evening, the visitor from England, had an identity Dr Barbara was at pains to hide, referring to him rather archly as 'Mr A' in her first autobiography and in her later account as, 'a doctor … an Anglo-Indian' or 'Mr P'. He was in fact Ardeshir Phirazsha Petigura, a British citizen born in India whose uncle was a senior official in the colonial government in India.

In her 1960 autobiography Dr Barbara admits to Ardeshir Petigura having rather more than a crush on her. Whether they were having an affair is a matter for conjecture. They first met in 1933 when Dr Barbara was having dinner at the Intourist Hotel in Moscow during one of her epic rides. No doubt she cut something of a striking figure with her long blonde hair and motorcycle gear. A smitten Ardeshir Petigura asked the head waiter who she was and then got him to introduce them. Petigura delayed his departure by several weeks in order to spend time with her and he travelled from Moscow to Leningrad where he stayed with Barbara and her husband. It is just possible that Dr Barbara was more interested in sex than she let on and it may be that her relationship with Ardeshir Petigura influenced the strategy Alexander Pataleev came up with to extract Barbara from her legal predicament.

His solution had echoes of his earlier plan when she was on the run in Volchansk. He suggested she should divorce him and marry Petigura. As the wife of a British citizen she would be entitled to a British passport. She could then leave the country and travel around Europe for a while then, when the trouble with General Uritzky had blown over, she could return, divorce Petigura and remarry Pataleev. Dr Barbara herself said that this was far from an ideal solution, yet she clutched at it like a drowning person might clutch at a straw.

It's hard to follow this logic. A cynic might view this plan as an unsubtle attempt by Alexander Pataleev to get his motorcycle and speed obsessed wife off his hands. In typical, mysterious 'Dr Barbara' style the events seem stunning, improbable and have no doubt been obscured by time and omission. She was almost certainly getting a little too close to Ardeshir Petigura and Alexander Pataleev may well have thought it was time for someone else to take over the duties of bailing Dr Barbara out whenever she got into trouble. Whatever the rationale all three of them filed into the Leningrad registry office one afternoon an hour before it was due to close. There Dr Barbara divorced Alexander Pataleev and married Ardeshir Phirazsha Petigura. The next day they went to the British Consulate where their marriage was registered and for the princely sum of fifteen roubles Dr Barbara Petigura received a British passport. Ardeshir Petigura, her husband of just one day, then left Russia for Europe.

She would never see him again.

Chapter Five: The Death Cell

THERE IS AN OLD SAYING, 'Marry in haste, regret at leisure.' For Dr Barbara and husband number two, Ardeshir Petigura, it was a case of marry in haste, regret almost immediately. If Dr Barbara had not been in enough trouble already, a week after her new marriage she was taken to GPU headquarters in Leningrad and told that she was now being considered a spy because Mr Petigura's uncle was not just a senior figure in colonial India, he was in charge of British Intelligence there. To further scupper her plans she was also told that even though she was now technically a British citizen and the holder of a British passport, she still might not be granted permission to leave Russia.

While this was happening, her new husband was quickly experiencing the realities of life being wedded to Dr Barbara. He travelled first to Berlin where, on Hitler's specific orders, he was expelled within twenty-four hours. Whether this had anything to do with his new Russian wife, his spymaster uncle or some other matter, remains unclear. He went next to Paris where the Sûreté expelled him, again within twenty-four hours. When he reached England his troubles were far from over. His hasty Soviet marriage seemed to have caused disquiet in the corridors of Whitehall as a breach of security if nothing else. His passport was confiscated and he was given a special explanatory note instead by way of a travel document and sent on an assignment to China and, if that wasn't enough, his intelligence chief uncle in India let it be known how angry he was at this new bride, accusing him of importing another Bolshevik spy into the British Empire. There were clearly a few unanswered questions about Dr Barbara's choice of second husband.

MEANWHILE BACK IN LENINGRAD, AFTER numerous delays, Dr Barbara's trial got underway. She was being tried for multiple traffic offences including the incident involving General Uritzky and the occasion when she broke the elderly woman's leg. Dr Barbara always maintained she never hit the old lady, rather that the latter fell over when she was trying to get out of the way of Dr Barbara's Harley-Davidson. The prosecution largely consisted of an alliance between the traffic militia, who considered her a menace on the roads, and General Uritzky. The one witness for the defence she was relying on, the policeman who had attended when she knocked the old lady over, had since died and although the courts would have provided her with legal counsel, she decided to conduct her own defence. She was supremely confident that there was really no case to answer. So much so that even though there was a chance she could be remanded in custody she took no toiletries or spare clothes with her. The trial jury took just forty-five minutes to find her guilty.

Given the serious nature of the case, the presiding judge (a woman) sentenced her to three years in prison; both of her motorbikes, the Harley-Davidson and the Indian, were to be confiscated; five years loss of civil and social rights; and a five year ban from driving upon release. For Dr Barbara it might as well have been a life sentence. She was taken from the courthouse, still dressed in her motorcycling clothes, straight to the women's prison in Leningrad.

DR BARBARA WAS A REMARKABLE person. She was intelligent, strong willed, had a huge capacity for hard work and a phenomenal commitment to achieve her objectives. It was this commitment and strength of will which had seen her train as both a doctor and as an engineer, and to not be thrown off course when others, jealous of her achievements and commitment, attempted to denounce her. That same strength of will enabled her to become a motorcycle champion and would, in the future, enable her to complete epic feats of marathon walking in Britain, Australia and the USA, when she was of an age when most people are thinking of slowing down. Yet despite all of this she didn't seem to think that the rules which governed everyone else should apply to her. She was a menace on the roads and had entered into an acrimonious dispute with a powerful Party official which she was never likely to win. Yet when these offences came home to roost she seemed to be in a state of denial and believed she was being unfairly treated. It was precisely in character that she refused to accept the ruling of the court.

For the first seven months of her sentence she was a model prisoner. She joined twenty other inmates in a large communal cell which was both Spartan yet comfortable. Along with the beds there was a table, a mirror, a sink, cooking facilities and even pictures hung on the walls. She began to make friends with the other female prisoners, while her now ex-husband Alexander Pataleev lodged numerous appeals on her behalf. She was truly a Soviet Heroine fallen from grace. The words of the judge, a spiteful and envious woman in Dr Barbara's eyes, were still ringing in her ears. 'What can you expect from a woman like Pataleeva, a former bourgeoisie?'

Most of her cell mates worked seven hours a day in the prison tailor shop and some were given three months leave away from jail to help bring in the harvest. As Dr Barbara had never worked on the land, couldn't sew, and had no intention of learning, she was given work driving a tractor around the prison grounds to move goods from the clothing factory or to take wood for the kitchen fires. The irony of this was not lost on her. She had been jailed for driving offences and then put to work in prison, driving.

After three months she was, somewhat unexpectedly, given a medical by the prison doctor and even though he was not supposed to tell her why, she wheedled the truth out of him. The prison authorities needed to know if she was strong and healthy enough to be sent to a lumber camp in the north of Russia to drive tractors there. This had echoes of her problems with the authorities in 1922 when the GPU wanted to send her to the Solovetsky Islands in the far north. Again she was determined this would not happen. It would be impossible, she reasoned, to petition for a review of her case if she was so far away from Leningrad. This time instead of faking suicide, she went on a hunger strike'unto death'.

Hunger strikes were forbidden in the Soviet Union and considered to be 'counter-revolutionary acts'. She sent a letter to the public prosecutor and the prison governor informing them that she would be refusing food and water for thirty days during which time she expected them to review her case. It caused something of a stir. For one thing, the Soviet legal system was supposed to be so robust, that miscarriages of justice were impossible; and also because if a prisoner died while on hunger strike the governor of the prison was held responsible and could even be subject to a custodial sentence himself. Despite this, the main reason for their concern was that when one prisoner began refusing food, copycat hunger strikes could spread through the prison like wildfire. This is exactly what happened.

With her earlier experience of fasting Dr Barbara found going on hunger strike much easier than most people would, certainly much easier than her cell mates. The prison authorities had not come across an inmate quite like her before, and despite all their urging and that of her fellow prisoners, most of whom abandoned their own attempts at hunger striking after the first few days, she was determined not to give in. Concerned that Dr Barbara's behaviour was bad for discipline in an overcrowded prison, and given that she was becoming weaker by the day, the governor made the decision to isolate her from the other prisoners. The only flaw with that strategy was that the women's prison in Leningrad had only eight isolation cells. They were in the basement and reserved for a special category of prisoner. But the authorities saw no alternative. Just four days into her hunger strike Dr Barbara was sent to the death cells.

HER NEW CELL MEASURED SIX feet by ten and had a small window with bars which let in very little light: death cells were in the basement. The bed was a wooden box filled with sand, thus too heavy for a prisoner to move, with a straw mattress and pillow on top.

Apart from Dr Barbara there were just two other inmates. These were Auntie Paraskovia, a middle-aged woman who had been convicted of stealing on an almost industrial scale from the textile factory where she worked, and 'Nyurka', a striking, twenty-one year old blue-eyed blonde, six foot tall; a gang leader and convicted murderer.

The cells were supposed to be locked and there was a guard posted outside at all times, but in practice they were never locked. Inmates were able to socialise as Dr Barbara quickly discovered when the imposing figure of Nyurka strode into her cell on the first day and demanded to know who she'd killed.

Neither Nyurka nor Auntie Paraskovia could understand what she hoped to achieve by going on hunger strike. Nyurka preferred to put her faith in either getting a pardon or hoping that her fellow gang members would be able to spring her from jail. She had already collected a number of improvised weapons, sharpened nails and slivers of glass, and hidden them under her mattress ready for a breakout. She became a regular visitor to Dr Barbara's cell and, possibly because Barbara, in her weakened state, could do little more than lie on her bed and listen, she would regale her with stories of her criminal adventures.

Shortly before her arrest Nyurka and her gang had been paid a substantial sum by an influential German consortium to steal a certain portfolio of important papers from the flat of a prominent Communist. Steal them they did, but in the process the Communist was killed. It was Nyurka herself who had smashed him in the temple with a hammer; then they had dismembered his body and hidden it under the flagstones in his cellar.

If the first week of her fast passed quite easily, as she entered the second week without food and water Dr Barbara began to feel very weak and her body started to show signs of wasting. Her gums began to recede, she constantly had an unpleasant taste in her mouth, her skin took on a greenish tinge and her death row companions told her that she was starting to smell like a corpse.

She was visited twice a day by the prison doctor and had regular visits from the governor and other government officials who tried everything, including leaving a plate of appetizing food at her bedside to tempt her to eat again. When her fast went beyond two weeks, matters began to get serious. It was evident that the prison authorities were genuinely concerned that in her weakened and emaciated state she might easily die, yet her extraordinary strength of will enabled her to keep going.

Dr Barbara couldn't help but become drawn into the culture of the death cells. The inmates never knew quite when they might receive a pardon, or be suddenly taken away for execution. The practice was that if it was a pardon they came for you during the day, but if it was for execution they came at night. Even the guards would try to be quiet during the hours of darkness and not let their keys jingle to avoid unnecessarily alarming the skittish death row prisoners.

On the fifteenth day of her hunger strike the door of Dr Barbara's cell flew open and Nyurka burst in telling her that they had come for her in the day. With tears streaming down her cheeks she kissed Barbara and told her she was to be released, then she dashed out to gather her things. It all proved to be a cruel trick. Knowing what a difficult and volatile customer Nyurka could be, the guards used this as a ruse to get her away from her cell. A few hours later she was shot.

After twenty-three days of hunger strike it was the authorities who blinked first. The governor received a message from Moscow:

'To the governor of Leningrad prison no. 8 Release Pataleewa immediately.'

Dr Barbara's sentence had been quashed and she was set free.

The death cells in Leningrad Women's Prison number eight were soon empty. Nyurka had been executed, Dr Barbara released, and a few days later Auntie Paraskovia faced the firing squad.

FOLLOWING HER RELEASE, AND AFTER a short period to build up her strength, Dr Barbara pressed ahead with her plans to leave Russia and tour Europe on her Motorbike. Even if in post-revolutionary Russia citizens were not free to travel abroad, she didn't think this rule should apply to her: especially as since her marriage to Ardeshir Petigura had made her technically a British citizen. She didn't see how they could stop her. After lengthy bureaucratic wrangling she was finally informed that she would be allowed to leave and to take her motorbike with her, but in order to do so her Russian citizenship would be revoked. If she left she would never be able to return to her beloved Russia.

It was a step into the unknown. She would be leaving her friends, family and Alexander Pataleev of course, the man who had done so much for her. She hoped that with the passage of time she would be able to secretly enter Russia again and be reunited with him. Yet she knew that once she was abroad she would have no help or support from anyone. Her new husband was unable to help her in the way that her first husband had done. He had his own problems, and besides he had been banished to China by the British government. For all she had flaunted its laws and had frequently fallen foul of the secret police she loved her native country and Russia remained her home. It was a massive wrench but she felt she had little option.

She climbed onto the Harley and rode across the border into Poland with tears flowing from her eyes and misting her motorcycle goggles so she could hardly see the road ahead. She left Russia behind forever and embarked upon a new chapter of her life.

Chapter Six: The Lost Years

DR BARBARA'S BROAD PLAN ON leaving Russia was to travel through Europe and then head for England. Once there she would arrange to divorce husband number two, Ardeshir Petigura. She considered this to be no more than a marriage of convenience, an arrangement on paper. After a short stay in Britain she would set out again to ride her motorbike through the Middle East, Egypt and on to India, a mystical country in her view and one she had wanted to visit since childhood. After touring India she planned to travel north to the Himalayan Mountains, the Hindu Kush, through the Khyber Pass and then cross secretly back into Russia where she could be reunited with Alexander Pataleev.

Wherever Dr Barbara went, trouble was never very far behind and her motorcycle tour through Europe proved to be almost as problematic as her previous life in Russia had been. She could only take what little gear she could carry on her bike, and because of currency export restrictions she wasn't allowed to take much money. Her greatest handicap however, given the volatility across Europe between the first and second World Wars, was that here she was a Russian woman, speaking only Russian, travelling on a British passport, riding an American motorbike, whose husband was the nephew of the man in charge of espionage in British India. Everywhere she went they took her to be a spy.

She rode her bike through Poland, Estonia, Latvia, Lithuania and Germany. In Germany she encountered problems with Hitler's border guards, when they found a hunk of gruyere cheese stowed in the Harley's tool box. It was wrapped up in an old crumpled copy of *Pravda*, the Russian newspaper, which had a picture of Stalin on it. She was accused of smuggling Communist literature, detained and strip searched.

From Germany she crossed into Switzerland, almost freezing to death on the high Alpine passes, and then into France. It was here that she had another run-in with border guards and customs officials when they demanded she pay £108 duty for 'triptyque' papers to export her bike to England. The only way she could avoid paying the exorbitant fee, one which she couldn't afford, was to cross back into Switzerland, park her bike there, and travel overland to England. There, as a British subject she could get the necessary 'triptyque' documents from the AA. Then she caught the ferry back to France, collected the Harley, and managed to be briefly arrested as a spy in Paris. On her release, and feeling she had successfully cocked-a-snook at the French authorities, she finally brought her bike to England where she set down shallow roots.

SHE SAID SHE LIKED THE English. She liked them for their politeness but didn't like their love of cats, greyhound racing or the football pools. Shortly after she arrived, and despite being hardly able to speak the language, she met and became friendly with the man who would later become her third husband, then an art student. They shared an interest in both motorbikes and vegetarianism.

She had hoped that it would be as easy to get a divorce in England from her second husband as it had been for her to divorce her first husband in Leningrad, but this proved not to be the case. Divorces were not readily granted in 1930s Britain and her husband being from India and subject to Indian legislation complicated matters still further. She was told she needed to go to India for the necessary legalities to be completed, even though her husband was not even in India at the time. At that point he was working as a doctor in China.

Dr Barbara now found herself stuck in England, a fledgling romance with Harry beginning to bloom but without the necessary funds to travel to India to get her divorce. She had no option but to find herself a job. Having trained as an engineer she was able to get work at the aircraft factory at Hanworth where she worked every bit of overtime she could in order to build up her cash reserves for her trip to India. She found a small flat in Twickenham and at weekends she and Harry would get together for a motorbike ride or, if she could get permission, to fly one of the planes from Hanworth Aerodrome. It was unlikely that a feisty and independent character like Dr Barbara would meekly submit to a regular work-a-day regime. She stuck it out for six months until the day she had a big row with the factory foreman. It seemed that her views and that of the factory management differed on the best way to assemble the wings of trainer aircraft. As she'd built up sufficient cash by then to fund her trip to India she threw in the job at Hanworth.

IT WOULD BE FAIR TO say that by this point in her life Dr Barbara was searching for something, a new focus, a mission, a goal of some sort, a quest, a degree of meaningfulness; something on which she could bring her considerable reserves of energy and willpower to bear. Her early life had been dominated by training to be a doctor then by her engineering and motorbike racing. Her life in Russia had turned sour with her arrest, imprisonment, her marriage to Ardeshir Petigura and her near fatal hunger strike. She was now prevented from returning to Russia so there was no possibility of picking up her old life again. She had found her travels through Europe interesting yet they were just a distraction: they did not fulfil her need for a sense of purpose.

Setting out from England on her Harley-Davidson she travelled through France, Spain, Persia and the Middle East and then via camel tracks and the Silk Road on to Bombay (now Mumbai) arriving in late 1935. Like many self-seekers before and after her, it would be in India that she would discover her new destiny.

Her primary reason for going to India was to get a divorce from her second husband. Again this proved to be no easy task. India is a place where the wheels of bureaucracy may turn but they grind on very slowly and it was clear she would have a long wait before she was free from her hastily arranged and ill thought out marriage. She spent three years travelling around by train and on her motorbike and letting the sights, smells and sounds of the sub-continent assail her senses. Part of the time she studied yoga in Bombay and part of the time she worked at a hospital in Bikaner, Rajasthan. Harry kept in touch by letter and would send her a little money whenever he could. One year he even managed to travel out by boat and they were able to spend ten days together.

IN 1937, SHE TRAVELLED NORTH to the Himalayas where she was able to see Kanchenjunga and Mount Everest from a distance. She also became lost amongst the hills in the dark and spent a cold and very scary night listening to the wolves howling all around. She would later, in 1953, offer her services to Sir John Hunt when he was gathering a team together for his successful assault on Mount Everest. If he had accepted her offer the history of mountaineering in the Himalayas may have been somewhat different. Instead he turned her down telling her his expedition was to be an all-male affair and besides she wasn't a member of the Alpine Club. He suggested she should apply to join a women's expedition. Rather nettled by his reply she said she could only climb with men, never with women. Even as late as 1960 she was still stating her intention to climb Everest, 'and I will do it on nothing but air,' she said, 'in such pure air my body could do anything, could live forever.'

IT WAS ON THIS TRIP to the mountains that she started to formulate her ideas of living on just pure air. In the foothills of the Himalayas she met two men living a simple life in a stone hut. They tended their flower garden and grew their own fruit and vegetables. She had a meal with them and they shared not only their food with her but also their philosophy of life. They ate just once a day, they said, and had done so for the last eighty years. This last statement came as such a shock to Barbara she almost choked on the piece of fruit she was eating. She couldn't believe they were more than eighty years old. She thought they were no more than in their mid-thirties. Both men appeared fit and healthy with glossy hair, bright eyes and strong teeth. After she left their hut she talked to the locals at the nearest village and they told her the two men were aged 116 and 119. She decided to stay on in the area determined to learn this new way of life from these two remarkable men. They lived on raw vegetables and fruit, most of which they grew themselves. They ate just once a day and had developed a specific way of breathing which apparently allowed them to gain sustenance from the clear air. Dr Barbara resolved to adopt a similar diet even though it would take her four and a half years of experimentation to perfect. Her experience in the mountains reawakened her earlier interest in health and diet and provided her with the sense of purpose and meaning in life which she had been seeking. After her visit to the Himalayas her life would be one long struggle of promoting this new Spartan diet, with a zeal which, at times, was almost evangelical in its intensity.

AFTER THREE YEARS, THE HEAT, the dust and the poverty of India was beginning to wear her down. She wanted to return to England, she wanted to see Harry and she wanted to work at developing her new dietary ideas. She was granted three months leave from the hospital where she was working and booked a passage back to the UK. Just before she was ready to leave she received a cable telling her that Harry had been involved in a motorcycle accident and was badly injured – dying.

The cable, which had been sent by Harry's parents, told her that such was the nature of Harry's injuries she shouldn't come back home but rather that she should stay in India. They had never approved of her relationship with Harry. She ignored them. Dr Barbara had to see her man. She sailed from Bombay on the P&O liner RMS Strathmore. When they reached the Mediterranean she persuaded the Captain to make an unscheduled stop at Monte Carlo so she could jump ship, catch an express train to Paris and then make a mercy dash to London.

She arrived at Victoria Station a day later having no idea where Harry was, what condition he was in, or even if he was still alive. One thing she was sure of was that if she tried to phone Harry's parents they would prevent her from seeing him. Ever resourceful Dr Barbara buttonholed the first intelligent looking stranger and asked him to phone Harry's parents, tell them he was a friend and, more importantly, ask *where* he was. They told the stranger he was alive and being treated in hospital just outside Nottingham. Leaving the stranger standing there she stashed her luggage at the station and jumped on the next train to Nottingham.

Still managing to fool Harry's parents she visited him in disguise. Dr Barbara's idea of a disguise was to put some lipstick on. He looked terrible. He'd sustained a skull fracture, had a nasty scar across his temple and was having difficulty getting his eyes to focus. Worse, from his and Dr Barbara's point of view, they were making him eat meat.

'Barbara, get me out of here!' he said.

His mother and father quickly became suspicious when staff on the ward told them about the strange foreign woman who'd visited him, yet Dr Barbara was undeterred. She was determined to get him away from the hospital and away from his parents.

It took her a few days to organise his liberation. First, she had to avoid his family and then for a brief time Harry was not allowed visitors when he was running a high temperature. Then one evening she was able to creep in during visiting time. Harry quickly pulled some clothes on over his pyjamas, and she smuggled him out of the ward and into a waiting taxi. Giving the driver instructions to head for London and not to stop for anything, they escaped. Dr Barbara had added kidnapping to her list of crimes and misdemeanours.

She took Harry first to a friend's flat in London and then after a few days, when he was well enough to travel, to the Hotel Winter in Paris's Latin Quarter. Harry was able to resume his vegetarian diet and slowly convalesce back to health. When they returned to London a few weeks later he was looking tanned and healthy. Dr Barbara's divorce papers had finally come through and, with the clouds of war gathering over Europe, they were married on 29th July 1939 at the Registry Office in Fulham, with a party afterwards for their friends back at Barbara's one room flat in Kensington.

This was the only one of her three marriages which Dr Barbara admits to being a marriage in a full and physical sense although she would in time revert to her previous celibacy. They went back to Paris for a honeymoon (the only one she'd ever had), then when war was declared they had a scramble to get back to England before the Nazi tanks rolled onto the Champs-Élysées.

THE SECOND WORLD WAR, FROM Dr Barbara's point of view, only started on 22nd of June 1941 when the Germans invaded her beloved Russia. Her father Vasilii Cherkasova was killed during an air raid near Saratov. The blast from a bomb threw the old man bodily into the air and he landed in a well. If it had been summer he may have survived but it was winter and the well was frozen. He sustained fatal injuries when he landed heavily on the ice.

Throughout the war Dr Barbara worked for the Ministry of Information giving lectures around the country on Russian affairs. She delivered more than 2,000 lectures and it was while she travelled around the country on tortuously slow railway journeys with endless waits on station platforms that she started to write her first autobiography, *I am a Woman from Soviet Russia*.

War time was a challenge to a staunch and committed vegetarian like Dr Barbara but a woman with her resolve was not going to let the little matter of a world war and nationwide rationing divert her from her principles. Once again it was an official government agency, the Ministry of Food this time, which had to back down when confronted with her iron will. She became one of only a handful of people who had no ration book and instead of meat and fats she was allowed honey, dried fruit and nuts.

HARRY HAD FINISHED AT ART school when the war ended and was soon earning a reasonable wage working as an art director in films. This enabled Dr Barbara to continue her dietary research. For the next twenty years she was busy experimenting with, and promoting the minimal vegetarian diet she had discovered from the two ancients in the foothills of the Himalayas. She wrote papers for journals such as the *Vegetarian Messenger* ('What's wrong with grass …') and *The Vegetarian News* ('The Bad Aspects of the English Diet'). She entered into heated debates with other prominent vegetarians as to whether her minimalist diet and eating just one meal a day was sufficient to sustain a normal person and she gave yet more talks and lectures. On 2nd April 1949 she addressed the London Vegan Group on the subject of 'My Experimental Fast'. She took issue with many aspects of a regular meat free diet such as eating the 'crunchy-munchy' type of breakfast cereal; 'one has to fight the ever increasing hypnosis of advertising magic'; or of eating 'heavy, soggy steamed puddings' which, she said, were quite likely to 'ruin any digestion, and set up a terribly constipated condition'. She counselled against 'the catarrh-promoting effects of milk puddings,' such as sago, tapioca or even one of the nation's favourites, rice pudding.

Whilst these debates were in themselves harmless, even if a little worrying that a trained medical doctor was promoting the view that a bowl of steamed duff would ruin the digestion, what was more concerning was that she furthered the idea of gaining nutrition from the special techniques of breathing which she had first encountered in the Himalayas. This was largely the concept of 'Breatharianism': living on sunshine and fresh air alone.

In all fairness to Dr Barbara Moore she never advocated the general adoption of the principles of Breatharianism, always arguing that an individual needed to be trained and to have accustomed their body over years of dietary control and fasting. And most publications or organisations which aim to highlight the benefits of Breatharianism add the rider that they take no responsibility for how individuals apply or use these principles. This is necessary because there is the very real danger that someone practicing this way of life in its purist form could starve to death. Yet Dr Moore was keen to showcase her Breatharianism principles highlighting how she would spend weeks in the Swiss mountains each year where the air was very pure. Once there she would eat nothing and only drink water from mountain streams or melted snow. On this diet she would climb in the Alps each day and walk fifteen to twenty miles to and from her hotel, never feel the cold or feel tired or hungry, and would only need three hours sleep.

'There is much more in sunlight and air,' she was quoted as saying. 'The secret is to find the way to absorb the extra – that cosmic radiation – and turn it into food.'

In 1952 she stayed at a spa in Austria where the waters were reputed to be radioactive. She didn't just take the waters, she drank them down in copious quantities. The following year she began to feel ill. She had a less than successful visit to the Alps that year; she felt a lack of energy, was lethargic and had difficulty concentrating. She flew home early to be greeted by the news that Harry had once again been involved in a serious motorbike accident. She had to quickly put aside her own problems to nurse him. Harry had suffered another fractured skull and his recovery was slow and at times very difficult. He was confused and sometimes violent. When he finally recovered, Barbara's earlier health problems began to reassert themselves. As a doctor Barbara felt able to diagnose her own illness. Drinking the excessive amounts of radioactive spa water in Austria had, she decided, caused her to develop leukaemia. She visited a specialist in Harley Street who confirmed her diagnosis: she was indeed suffering from leukaemia. He gave her just six months to live.

For Barbara the ignominy of her, a vegetarian for almost all of her life and active advocate of a pure and healthy diet, dying from leukaemia was almost as bad as the prospect of death itself. She travelled to Switzerland again as she had done each summer, supposedly for a heath cure, but in reality she was planning her own death. She planned to climb a high mountain and leap off a precipice, but somehow she could never bring herself to do it. Each day she would return to her hotel intent on suicide the next day. When she flew back to England she was so weak Harry had to meet her at the airport to take her home.

Once home Dr Barbara drew the curtains and didn't leave her house for four years. She didn't sleep. She hardly ate and, apart from one set of clothes, gave everything else away. She wouldn't allow anyone to visit her. She withdrew totally.

The six months the Harley Street consultant had given her passed. 'I was still alive,' she said. 'But I was not *living*.' She was existing on just Malvern water and fruit juice, trying to focus all she had learnt in the Himalayas to combat the cancer in her blood. She received the news that the Harley Street doctor who had confirmed her diagnosis had died. Still Dr Barbara remained locked away in a silent, dark house. Her self-imposed isolation even gave rise to rumours amongst the neighbours that Harry had done away with her and hidden her body in the garden. Still she remained at home. The woman who had faked her own death in the Volga River, become motorcycle champion of the Soviet Union, ridden her Harley-Davidson singlehandedly across Europe, had roared across India and high into the Himalayas, hid herself away from the world.

After four years of self-imposed isolation she began to believe that the leukaemia was passing, that she had defeated it. She felt as if she had emerged from a long and very dark tunnel into the sunlight at last. She started to feel well again and with it her confidence and energy returned. Once more she felt able to pick up her struggle from where she had been forced to leave off; to continue her mission, her fight to prove the superiority of her minimalist vegetarian diet.

The balance of probability is that despite drinking the supposedly radioactive spa water, Dr Barbara never suffered from leukaemia. Self-diagnosis, even for a trained healthcare professional, is a hazardous business. The Harley Street specialist, if indeed he ever existed, rather conveniently dropped out of the picture, so we only have her subjective account of events. Her symptoms: the suicidal ideas, poor sleep, loss of appetite, withdrawal from the world, all following the trauma of her husband's life-threatening motorbike accident, point towards the strong likelihood that Dr Barbara had suffered from depression rather than leukaemia.

For Dr Barbara, with her revolutionary dietary theories, overcoming life-threatening leukaemia became yet another part of the myth, another chapter in her remarkable story. But for all of her extreme ideas on diet and her claims that one day she hoped to live 'entirely on air', these arguments and debates had little impact on a wider public. They were confined to a relatively small circle of individuals who had a specific interest in matters of nutrition and pushing the boundaries of diet. Dr Moore was seen as a likable crank; an eccentric from overseas with quirky views about diet and life who nobody took seriously. Not, that is, until she started entering marathon walks and posting times which men half her age struggled to equal. Suddenly Dr Barbara Moore and her remarkable diet were news and the world had to listen to what she was saying.

Chapter Seven: Groats End

BACK IN JANUARY 1960 IT would have been very easy for the regular newspaper reader to reach the conclusion that Dr Barbara Moore was the only person in Britain setting out on mammoth walks. Yet this was far from the truth. Despite it being the depths of winter, the marathon walking craze was in full swing and the keenest walkers had ambitions which extended beyond the modest 110 miles between Birmingham and Marble Arch. They set their sights on what was considered to be the ultimate British walk: from one end of Great Britain to the other. John O'Groats, that tiny community in the far north-east of Scotland where the ferries leave to the Orkney Islands, to Land's End, the rocky headland jutting out into the Atlantic Ocean on the south-west tip of Cornwall.

Joseph Dixon, a forty-six year old welder from Yorkshire set out on the same day as Dr Barbara. Dorothy Scott, a forty-six year old widow from Liverpool set out a day later. She was presented with eight pounds by Liverpool MP Bessie Braddock to help towards her expenses. Scott would later give the Butlin race organisers something of a headache when they were unable to establish whether she was in the race or not. Later still she would style herself as Britain's answer to Dr Moore and set off on her own odyssey, a 4,328 mile hike around the coast of Britain.

Peter Hoy, a TV actor from Manchester and Keith Symington, a building foreman from Southport, had left a day earlier and Liverpool sisters Wendy and Joy Lewis were approaching the border having set out nine days earlier with none of the fuss or media hype which accompanied Dr Barbara. Here the newspapers missed a trick. While they focused almost exclusively on Dr Moore, eighteen year old Wendy Lewis had slipped under the media's radar. In a few short weeks she would become a star in her own right, the poster girl of the Billy Butlin Race, and she would steal Dr Barbara's crown along with the hearts of the nation.

LIFE IN BRITAIN IN 1960 was very different to Britain after the Millennium. The Second World War still cast a long shadow and austerity was a fact of life. Food rationing had only ended six years before in 1954, and National Service for men only would only end later in 1960. The last National Service soldier was not demobbed until 1963.

There had been a huge population explosion after the war, when returning servicemen quickly married and started families, the so-called Baby Boom. People were generally respectful and deferential to those in authority, such as teachers, politicians and ministers of religion. Bankers in the City of London all wore Bowler hats, dark jackets, striped trousers and carried a rolled-up umbrella when they went to work. Shops closed at lunchtime and for half-day closing one day each week, usually a Wednesday afternoon. The Church of England ensured that Sundays remained a religious day when shops were not allowed to open. There were no sporting events such as football or horse racing on Sundays and in some parts of the country they even locked and chained up the swings in children's playgrounds. In Wales no alcohol at all was sold on a Sunday.

Harold Macmillan (Super Mac) was the Conservative Prime Minister. The previous October he had won a third consecutive victory, with an increased majority. Dwight D. Eisenhower (Ike), who had been a five star general in the US Army during World War II, was the Republican President in America.

The first section of the M1 motorway between Watford and Rugby had opened the previous November but only thirty percent of British households owned a car. The average weekly wage was £14.10 (or £14/2shillings as it was pre-decimalisation). Ian Fleming published the James Bond thriller *Goldfinger* and, quite appropriately in view of the recent marathon walking craze, Alan Sillitoe published the *Loneliness of the Long Distance Runner*.

BEFORE DR MOORE COULD START out from John O'Groats, a new row had erupted about whether her time of seven days, twelve hours and five minutes for her 373 mile walk from Edinburgh to London had truly been bettered. On 5th January 1960 Terry Haywood, a lorry driver from Birmingham, claimed to have covered the distance in six days, one hour and fifteen minutes, without suffering as much as a blister. This prompted Dr Barbara to throw down a challenge to him of walking John O'Groats to Land's End with her. Mr Haywood declined her offer, and instead was photographed being presented with a cheque for £250 by garage owner Wilfred McDougall, from Bilson in Staffordshire.

They told the *Daily Mail* that neither of them liked walking very much. Here was a curious thing, almost all of the participants in this new marathon walking craze claimed that they *didn't* enjoy walking. Paratrooper Staff Sergeant Mervyn Evans, who along with his friend Flight Sergeant Patrick Maloney, could reasonably claim to have started off this whole craze, said he'd sooner do a parachute jump for each mile rather than walk. Billy Butlin said that whenever he felt the urge to exercise he'd found the best policy was to go and have a 'lay down until the feeling wears off;' and even Dr Barbara Moore herself, the woman who was now synonymous with marathon treks, claimed that next time she went from John O'Groats to Land's End she'd do it by 'fast car.' The question was, did Terry Haywood's dislike of walking prompt him to take a lift for part of the way? On the 6th January, Bob Stenhouse, a laundry van driver from Jedburgh, claimed to have given Terry Hayward a lift for some eight miles, dropping him off in Jedburgh marketplace.

Bob Stenhouse said he was alerted to something being wrong when Terry Haywood was reluctant to chat or answer the usual questions you would ask a hitch-hiker. Things like, 'Where have you come from?', 'How far are you going?' and 'are you going to stay in Jedburgh tonight?'

'I took special notice of the hitch-hiker's appearance,' he told the *Daily Mail*. '… [H]e did not talk very much and I was suspicious. He was wearing a black plastic mac, khaki drill trousers and gloves. Today I saw a picture of Haywood in a newspaper and I am sure he was the man I picked up.'

Dr Barbara, not usually known for her reticence, was careful not to accuse Terry Haywood of cheating but she clearly remained sceptical, especially about his claim not to have even raised a blister on his walk. 'I don't accuse him of fraud,' she said, 'I just say that he did not do it the same way that I did.'

The matter was never fully resolved. It was a case of Haywood's word against van driver Bob Stenhouse, and a lift of just eight or nine miles is unlikely to have accounted for him taking more than a day off Dr Barbara's time. Given the unregulated nature of these walks it was probably impossible to prove whether Terry Haywood had won the race fairly or not. As soon as these accusations were made he promised not to cash his £250 cheque until his name had been cleared. A few days later on 12th January the *Sheffield Telegraph* reported that Mr Haywood was 'not interested in cashing the prize cheque'. Later the same day the *Sheffield Star*, reporting on Peter Hoy and Keith Symington's End to End trek, quoted Peter Hoy's approach to big walks: 'I always like to estimate on the outside, like I did when I broke the record between Edinburgh and London.' Clearly Peter Hoy believed himself to be the holder of the Edinburgh to London record.

While the newspapers were arguing over whether or not Terry Haywood took a lift for less than ten miles, nothing was being said about a much more blatant piece of kidology. The media across the board trumpeted Dr Barbara's walk, and later the Billy Butlin Walk from John O'Groats to Land's End as 1,000 miles, overstating the distance by more than ten percent.

Dr Barbara herself estimated her walk at 1,000 miles. The starting point for her calculations was an AA route card which set the distance at 865 miles, but this was using ferries. As she didn't intend to use ferries she rounded the figure up to 1,000 miles, clearly an overestimation. Dr Barbara Moore and the Billy Butlin walkers covered 891 miles on their trek which, considering road changes, is probably a shorter distance than could be walked today. Brian Smails, in his book *John O' Groats to Land's End: The Official Challenge Guide* suggests that 900 miles is the shortest practical distance on public roads. A green route, following footpaths and byways and avoiding roads wherever possible, is usually somewhere in the region of 1,200 miles. The author's walk from Land's End to John O'Groats (completed in stages between 2008 and 2010, see *LE-JOG-ed: A Mid-lifer's Trek from Land's End to John O'Groats*) was longer still at 1,270 miles. The distance indicated on the signposts at both Land's End and John O'Groats is 874 miles but a trek of 1,000 miles makes for much better headlines. Even the signposts were changed for the Billy Butlin Walk.

WITH ALL OF THESE CONTROVERSIES flying around in the media it was probably something of a relief for Dr Moore to set off walking, which she did, from John O'Groats at dawn on 13th January 1960. Her progress was reported each day in the press. The gallant, exotic and rather mysterious Dr Babs, dressed in her blue tracksuit, plimsolls and sheepskin coat, tramped ever southwards impervious to the wind, rain, sleet or whatever the Scottish elements could throw at her. Through all of this she was sustained by just raw vegetables, nuts and fruit juice, proving, in her eyes at least, the benefits of this healthy if uninspiring diet. A diet which the average Englishman at the time would not have considered sufficient to even keep him on his legs. It was the sort of quirky, eccentric story lapped up by newspaper readers as welcome relief amongst the usual gloomy January news. Dr Babs was everything the nation liked; the plucky underdog sticking to her principles in the face of ridicule and opposition. Seeing off her challengers, especially the men, and showing them that she could do it and that she wasn't a cheat or a fraud. The public loved her for it and cheered her every mile of the way.

When she passed through Wick, the first town south of John O'Groats, the girls' pipe band turned out to play and escort her through the streets. On day two of her walk she'd reached Berriedale, but with almost fifty miles walked her ankle was starting to give her problems. On 15th January she took a brief rest at Dingwall and three days later she was battling through headwinds and atrocious weather trudging ever southwards. On 21st January, whilst amongst a throng of spectators she was accidently kicked on the ankle which, along with her knee, started to give her trouble.

Prior to her walk she had had to fend off somewhere in the region of fifty requests by people wanting to join her, offers from the UK and abroad, from sportsmen, adventurers, and even one from a West End actor. She refused all-comers saying that it was *her* challenge and she would prove what 'miracles' her diet could produce.

However, she couldn't stop the reporters who were keen to walk alongside her. The *Daily Mirror's* 'Cassandra' walked along with her for five miles through the driving rain outside Glasgow. He was filled with admiration not only for her courage and determination but also for her fitness, turn of speed and 'long loping stride'. A 'walk of wackiness', he called it, a 'delight of daftness', undertaken by a 'terrific woman … she terrifies and entrances me … her triumphal, dominant …[and] slightly pathetic march down the spine of Great Britain.' Here he effectively summed up what was becoming the biggest frustration for Dr Moore. While she clearly enjoyed her celebrity and the media attention, she was making these walks to demonstrate what she believed to be a serious, valid and scientific point, the superiority of her rigorous vegetarian diet which she had discovered in the Indian foothills of the Himalayas. Her walks, she believed, made this point and she wanted to be taken seriously. The press, on the other hand, wanted to show her as the quirky eccentric. Much of her later behaviour and her general falling out with the press should be seen in this light. As many a short-lived celebrity have found out to their cost, the media will build them up in the eyes of the public only to dash them down and humiliate them just a few months later. In Dr Barbara's case *The People* would soon be calling her 'that crazy woman' and before the summer was out she would be the *Daily Mail's* 'bore of the month'.

IN THE BRITAIN OF THE late 1950s and early 1960s vegetarianism was looked upon with some misgivings. Most people stuck to the traditional meat and two veg English diet. Even foreign food was viewed with suspicion and mistrust.

Vegetarianism, far from being main-stream was associated with an alternative lifestyle and radical views often linked with anti-establishment figures such as playwright George Bernard Shaw or Mahatma Gandhi. Even *The British Vegetarian* magazine in its 1959 Summer edition conceded that, 'Vegetarians are frequently described as "odd" as "cranks" and the like …', and Dr Moore's ideas on diet were radical, even for vegetarians of the day. A punishing exercise regime such as walking John O'Groats to Land's End in twenty three days, in the depths of winter on a diet of just nuts, fruit juice and honey would be questionable to vegetarians and meat eaters alike. But to the vegetarian movement in the 1950s and 60s she was a godsend. They delighted in her achievements. Here was living, breathing and, more importantly, walking proof of just what could be achieved on a meat free diet. Under the headline of 'Walking to Fame' *The British Vegetarian* trumpeted her achievements walking Birmingham to Marble Arch (twice) and 373 miles from Edinburgh to London describing her walks as 'heroic' and claiming that she had 'provided more good propaganda for the efficacy of vegetarianism than most of us do in a life-time.'

However not all vegetarians welcomed Dr Barbara's extreme views on diet even if she was good for publicising the cause. Nolan Highton, the proprietor of one of London's top vegetarian restaurants, was keen to present a more normalised view of a meat free diet. 'The trouble is,' he said, 'a very small minority of vegetarians are cranks [yet] they make a terrible noise.'

In March 1960 her achievements made her the toast of the British Vegetarian Society. In front of a capacity crowd in Kensington Town Hall, and amid much pomp and ceremony, they presented her with a specially minted gold medal to recognise her 'magnificent walks.'

Even after she fell from grace, the vegetarian movement in Britain still maintained a touching regard for her. In his obituary for her published in the *New Vegetarian* in July 1977, Edward Banks described her as 'The Amazing Dr Babs ... one of the most remarkable women of recent times.' And few could honestly challenge this view.

BY THE END OF JANUARY 1960 some of the walkers who had set out before Dr Barbara were beginning to arrive at Land's End. Actor Peter Hoy and builder's foreman Keith Symington, who had left the day before Dr Barbara, reached Land's End having taken nineteen days and fourteen hours. They said they were not competing with her, yet it was clear that Dr Barbara resented anyone sharing the media spotlight with her. On the 1st February she met walker Julian Nelson, a forty-one year old unemployed aircraft worker, on the road. He was heading north walking in the opposite direction and was clearly more pleased to meet her than she was to see him. 'You will never get there,' she told him bluntly as he approached. And then went on to pass her expert judgement on his walk. 'I've been studying your stride as you came along. My advice is to give up and get yourself a job.'

She was also scathing about walkers who competed in marathon treks where there was a financial reward. Peter Hoy and Keith Symington shared an £800 prize which had been funded by a department store. Dr Barbara considered she had a higher calling, using herself as a human guinea pig. Her walks were to prove to the world her theories about the superiority of a vegetarian diet.

Sisters Wendy and Joy Lewis from Liverpool, who were not walking for prize money, had mixed fortunes on their walk. They set off nine days before Dr Barbara and Wendy arrived at Land's End on 7th February, three days after Dr Moore's triumphant arrival. A septic foot, which needed hospital treatment, forced twenty-three year old Joy to retire at Oakhampton, having covered 900 miles; eighteen year old Wendy had to carry on alone. They maintained they were not trying to compete with Dr Barbara. For one thing they didn't have a van along to support them so were unable to walk at night. Wendy was astonished to be greeted by huge crowds at Land's End, a reception which almost rivalled Dr Moore's.

Wendy Lewis had no interest in the dietary issues which Dr Moore was promoting. 'I eat anything,' she said, when questioned by the *Daily Mail*. When asked why she undertook the walk she said, 'Because Dr Moore was planning the trip and I thought that what a middle-aged Russian woman could do, a teenage English girl could do just as well. We set out to prove that teenagers are not softies and layabouts who want to do nothing except have cheap fun.'

Dr Moore reportedly commented later that Wendy Lewis was a hitchhiker, not a walker. Wendy responded by challenging Dr Moore to a race back to John O'Groats.

WITH ALL OF THE MEDIA and public attention it must have been difficult at times for Dr Barbara Moore to stay focused on her walk. The fact that she was walking along public roads made her easily accessible to the public and they turned out in their thousands to cheer her on. Lorry drivers would wind down their windows and shout encouragement, motorists honked their horns, workers in factories left their benches and came out into the road to applaud her and children ran out with autograph books for her to sign. Every self-respecting youngster in those days had an autograph book and they vied with one another to collect the signatures of top sports stars and celebrities of the day. In January 1960 there was no bigger star than Dr Barbara Moore. The public related to her and to the long distance marching craze. It was *their* walk and she was *their* Dr Babs. Concerned about her being

61

overwhelmed by the crowds, at one point the police provided her with an escort, and she outpaced them. Even serious floods in Gloucestershire couldn't stop her. She swapped her famous plimsolls for a pair of Wellington boots and pressed on through the water.

On 1st February 1960, shortly after the Gloucester floods, the *Daily Mail* reported a new drama: "Find my husband", pleads Dr Babs'. Harry Moore had arrived near Bristol to see her but the redoubtable Dr Barbara would not let him walk along with her. She said he slowed her down. Just a little miffed, Harry left her to it and took himself off for a cup of tea. Sometime later, when she wanted him, he was nowhere to be found. They managed to meet up a short while later at the police station in Bristol where poor Harry was in for an ear-bashing because of the delay *he'd* caused.

Despite generating considerable favourable publicity for vegetarianism, Dr Barbara's extreme views on diet and her tendency to Breatharianism were never far from the surface. As she approached Bodmin Moor in Cornwall she commented to *Daily Mail* reporters that she had been losing weight at the rate of a pound and a half per day and how she found this puzzling. For someone walking more than 40 miles a day continuously for twenty-two days and eating only fruit, vegetables and nuts it was not surprising that she was losing weight, yet medically trained Dr Barbara attributed her weight loss to smoke and dirty air. 'Now I'm back in the fresh air of Devon and Cornwall,' she said, 'I'll probably start putting weight on again.'

AT 5.40 ON THE MORNING of 4th February 1960, after a light breakfast of grapefruit salad, bananas and Cornish clotted cream (she was deep in the West-Country after all), Dr Barbara Moore set out from Bodmin with sixty-two miles still to go.

Dr Barbara Moore with husband Harry.

The day turned into something of a carnival and she succeeded in single-handedly bringing Cornwall to a standstill. Thousands lined her route to cheer her along. Crowds of 7,000 were reported at Penzance and 15,000 in Cambourne. Work stopped in local factories, councilors postponed a meeting of the West Penwith Rural Council so they could go out to show their support, and she caused a five mile traffic jam at Redruth. Bands played and children gave her flowers. Weary, footsore, her cardigan carelessly buttoned one up and one down yet still walking with a spring in her step, the indomitable Dr Barbara Moore arrived at a floodlit Land's End at 11.25 in the evening amidst the cheering crowds and rockets being fired into the air. As she was mobbed by the excited crowd some even tried to snatch bits of her kit or her clothing to keep as a souvenir.

'I never realised how much this walk meant to the people of this country,' she said when interviewed. 'I have been cheered by the tremendous kindness and sympathy, particularly this last day. Now I would like a good night's sleep.'

Even in her moment of triumph she remained true to her diet. When she joined local civic leaders for a banquet at the Land's End Hotel her meal consisted of melon cocktail, vegetable soup and a 'fast-walker' salad, followed by pineapple and ice-cream for sweet.

'I started this walk to set an example,' she said. 'I believe healthier, saner, cleaner living can only come through sensible diet.'

DR BARBARA MOORE MAY HAVE been eccentric, attention-seeking and at times uncharitable, yet walking almost 900 miles from John O'Groats to Land's End in twenty-three days in the depths of the winter – as a fifty-six year old on a diet of just fruit, nuts and honey – was, by anyone's standards, a phenomenal achievement. And the British public loved her for it.

As she was finally able to put her feet up at Land's End, Britain's most high profile, flamboyant and innovative entrepreneur of the day was in his Mayfair apartment reading the newspaper reports of her success with more than just a passing interest. Billy Butlin thought the matter over while he took his morning bath, then he put on his habitual grey double-breasted suit, linen shirt and silk tie, and headed for his office in Oxford

Street. As soon as he arrived, he called his executive management team together for an extraordinary meeting.

'We are going to organise the walk to end all walks,' he told them. 'A race from John O'Groats to Land's End. We start now.'

Chapter Eight: The Birth of a Showman

IT WOULD BE HARD TO overstate the public profile of Billy Butlin in Britain in the 1950s and 1960s. The concept of Reality TV was still a few decades in the future yet if programs like *Dragons' Den* or *The Apprentice* had been on the nation's television screens back then it wouldn't have been Lord Alan Sugar sitting behind the boardroom table, pointing a finger at some hapless contestant and barking, 'You're Fired!' It would have been Mr Holiday Camps himself. He was the Lord Sugar, Sir James Dyson, and Sir Richard Branson of his day, all rolled into one rather rotund package.

Billy Butlin, the holiday camp entrepreneur was, in the words of his biographer Rex North, the 'man who had grown rich by selling happiness'. He was a man who started from the humblest of origins. The term 'a self-made man' could have been coined especially for him.

MUCH LIKE THE OLD MUSIC hall joke about the vicar and the showgirl, Billy's parents were the most unlikely and miss-matched couple. His father came from a long line of well-to-do clergymen. His mother Bertha was daughter of a showman who worked the fairs around the West Country of England and, in the best traditions of the travelling show folk, she had been born in a caravan.

Shortly after they married the couple emigrated to South Africa and it was there in Cape Town that William Edmund Colbourne Butlin was born in 1899. Billy's father was, by all accounts, something of a charmer. He was also an excellent tennis player and quickly became the grass court champion of Cape Town. Sadly he was less adept at providing for his family. They established a business assembling and selling bicycles from parts imported from England, but it was never really successful. After five years the marriage was over and Bertha returned to England with Billy, leaving her husband behind in South Africa.

When he first arrived in England the young Billy spoke Afrikaans as his first language. He had no proper schooling and, as Bertha returned to her life amongst the show people, they led a nomadic existence travelling with a fairground around the country and living in a gipsy caravan pulled by an old horse called Blackbird. Billy looked back on this romantic lifestyle as an idyllically happy time for him.

In 1911 Bertha remarried and emigrated again. This time she crossed the Atlantic to Canada, where she settled in Toronto with her new husband. Billy stayed behind with Bertha's family and the show people initially, and joined his mother and step-father two years later, when he was twelve. School still held little appeal for the young Butlin; he left as early as he could and found himself a job, albeit a poorly paid one. First, he was employed collecting wastepaper, and then he moved to Eatons Department Store where he worked as an office boy. This early period of his life in Canada was to prove important for him because it was there that he first encountered the holiday camps which would later make his fortune. Canadians would take their vacations in specially constructed camps amongst the lakes and forests. They would live in log cabins where their meals and lots of holiday activities, such as swimming, hiking and fishing, were all available in the same backwoods location.

Fifteen year old Billy, though small for his age, volunteered for the Canadian army at the outbreak of the First World War. This was an attempt to impress his girlfriend. He confidently expected to be turned down pretty quickly on account of his age and size, so he was stunned to be told by a hoary old recruiting sergeant to report back the following day to be kitted out with his uniform. He was so small in those days the hem of his army greatcoat would drag along the ground when he walked.

It would be fair to say that after this inauspicious start the young Billy Butlin and the Canadian army were never going to be a match made in heaven. He tried to desert; they threw him in the glasshouse. He overstayed his leave; they took away his lance-corporal's stripe. Nonetheless he served in the trenches in France amongst all the muck and bullets, the death and destruction. When the conflict was over he was demobbed back to Canada.

Like most soldiers Billy didn't find it easy to settle back to civilian life. What appealed to him most was the memory of those years travelling around England with his mother, living in a caravan and working the fairgrounds. In 1921 he decided to leave Canada for good. He shipped out of Newfoundland and worked his passage in a cattle boat bound for Liverpool where he landed with just five pounds in his pocket. In a little over twenty-five years he would have turned that fiver into a fortune and made himself a millionaire by building his holiday camp empire from scratch.

Billy hitchhiked his way to Dorney's Yard just outside Bristol. This was the overwintering spot for West Country travelling fairs, where they would freshen up, paint and repair their sideshows and caravans for the coming season. He was taken in by his aunt, Lottie Connolly, who arranged a bunk for him in one of the caravans and helped set him up with a hoop-la stall.

Once he had a business of his own, albeit something as modest as a hoop-la stall, his natural entrepreneurial flair began to come to the fore. He painted his stall blue and yellow, his favourite colours, colours which would later become synonymous with Butlin's. He made it look as bright, cheerful, and showy as he could, and made sure his name 'Butlin' was prominently displayed. When he was working behind his stall he would always wear a crisp white coat with the letter 'B' embroidered on the breast pocket. Even in those early days he understood that in show business it is colour, glitz and dazzle which sells.

But there was more to Butlin's hoop-la stall than just surface gloss. A factor which would later play a major part in making his holiday camps a success was that he tried to make sure his customers always got a good deal. Fairground sideshows were, and indeed many still are, notorious for being, if not quite crooked, at the very least having the odds stacked heavily in favour of the stall holder rather than the punter. Shooting ranges where the rifle barrels are out of true; or coconut shies where it would take something more like a howitzer shell to dislodge the coconut. Butlin experimented with his hoop-la stall and found that no matter how skilfully you threw the hoop it was all but impossible to win. The prizes stood on rectangular wooden blocks and in order to win the prize the hoop had to go over both the prize and the wooden block. Winning was practically impossible. Billy decided to make the blocks smaller to give the customer more of a sporting chance. It was a move which, not for the first time, would throw him into conflict with authority. A row ensued. The leaders of the fairground told him in no uncertain terms he was 'there to take money *off* the punters, not to give it away.' But young Billy stood his ground. He ignored these older and supposedly wiser heads. He stuck with the smaller wooden blocks and when the fair opened he did a roaring trade. He gave away a lot more prizes than the other stalls, but in turn he had a lot more customers and he raked in a lot more cash.

Butlin's fairground business expanded rapidly, he began employing others to work the stalls for him and was soon able to bring his mother, now widowed, over from Canada to help run his expanding empire. After nine years he was running the fairground for Bertram Mills' Circus at Olympia every Christmas, and he had established the biggest amusement park on the east coast, at Skegness in Lincolnshire.

One of the drawbacks of Skegness at that time was that to walk from the promenade to the sea involved a laborious trudge across a soft beach. Billy set out to improve the holiday maker's lot by building a boardwalk over the sand. No doubt he should have gone through the official channels before doing this, made a planning application to the local council and coped with the inherent bureaucracy and the inevitable delays. Hooper's Law states that it is always easier to act and then apologise after the event than to get permission beforehand, so Billy just went ahead and built the boardwalk. He built it from the promenade to the sea *but with just a sight detour via his amusement park*. The footfall of his amusement park rapidly increased, along with his profits. The local council responded, some weeks later. Far from removing what had become a very popular walkway, they made it a permanent concrete path.

Holiday makers at that time stayed in boarding houses which were presided over by fearsome and all-powerful landladies. The idea of the customer always being right, or of leaving a review on *Trip-Advisor* were still years away. The caricature of the seaside dragon landlady were the frequent butt of music hall jokes and McGill-type postcards. They ruled their boarding houses with a rod of iron. You had to be on time for meals, or you missed them. You were turned out after breakfast, no matter what the weather was doing, and some even imposed a nine o'clock curfew in the evenings. If the weather was bad, families would have a dreary and expensive holiday cast out of their boarding house as the wind and rain lashed the promenade. The only forms of shelter were cafes, pubs or amusement arcades all of which took a heavy toll on their holiday money. Landladies could get away with this because in the pre-World War II era people were less independent and more ready to submit to authority figures, and because there was simply no competition. Billy Butlin watched the bedraggled holiday makers as they traipsed around through the rain and thought back to the holiday camps he had visited in Canada. They were a concept unknown in Britain at the time; a holiday complex with simple chalet-type accommodation, all meals and all the entertainments provided onsite for the 'campers,' and all of this at a price which working people could afford.

In 1936 Billy Butlin revolutionised the holiday industry in Britain when, in the space of just one winter, he turned a turnip field near the Lincolnshire village of Ingoldmells into the first holiday camp in Britain: Butlin's Skegness. It was sensationally popular.

Not only did Butlin combat the dourness of the seaside landlady by providing 'all found' holidays he also employed his famous Redcoats as camp hosts, to make sure everyone joined in the fun, and he booked the top acts of the day to entertain his campers.

Butlin, ever the 'hands on' manager, was the face and personality who embodied his Holiday Camp Empire. He was 'Mr Holidays' himself, 'the man who sold happiness'. In appearance, he was short and stockily built, with a narrow pencil moustache, sometimes referred to as a 'Ronald Coleman' moustache, along his top lip. He was always smart and well turned out, usually in a double-breasted suit.

Butlin's Skegness was quickly a roaring success which he consolidated by importing yet another good idea from Canada, Dodgem Cars. He remembered what a fairground favourite they had been and working on the principle of 'where there's a laugh there's a shilling' he introduced Dodgems to Britain and maintained what was a very lucrative agency for their sale across Europe.

Skegness was quickly followed by a new camp at Clacton. This coincided, in 1938, with the *holidays-with-pay* movement in Britain when it became the law for all workers to get a week's paid holiday. Butlin responded to this hugely fortuitous set of events with the slogan:

'Holidays with pay – Holidays with play.' And he hired a V.I.P train to bring every M.P. who had supported the holidays-with-pay movement to the opening of the new Clacton Camp.

It would be easy to suggest that Billy Butlin benefited from incredible good fortune when holidays-with-pay became law just as his camps were taking off and up to a point this would be true. But as Colonel 'Elephant' Bill Williams (who would later play a significant part in the 'Big Charlie' episode) commented, 'His [Billy Butlin] was the story of a man, not so much lucky as capable of recognising when opportunity knocked on his door.' Yes, Butlin did well from the holidays-with-pay legislation, but he was far from the only player in the holiday industry: yet few capitalised on it in the way he did. He came up with a new slogan: 'A week's holiday for a week's wage.' This, along with his phenomenal organisational abilities, was at the heart of his success. He spotted an opportunity and made the most of it to the benefit of his holiday camp empire and he would do this again and again by organising or participating in well-publicised events which would engage the interest of the public at large while raising the profile of his holiday camps. Events such as: the Cross Channel Swim, the 'rescue' of Big Charlie, the Blériot Air Race and of course, the 'race to end all races' from John O'Groats to Land's End.

By the late 1930s Butlin's camps and holidays-with-pay were proving a great success and things were looking up for the lad who had arrived from Canada with just five pounds in his pocket. But across Europe the political landscape was looking grim with the looming threat of Nazism. When the Second World War broke out the fun had to stop for the duration when the government requisitioned Butlin's camps to use as training bases for the armed forces.

Butlin's first camp at Skegness was taken over by the Royal Navy for training and recruitment and, in keeping with naval tradition, they renamed it as HMS Royal Arthur. Once, and much to the amusement of old Butlin hands, it became the target of Nazi propaganda when the traitor William Joyce, better known as Lord Haw-Haw, announced in a radio broadcast that the battle ship HMS Royal Arthur had been torpedoed and sunk with all hands.

The wartime government quickly learnt to use the organisation skills of a man who could transform a muddy turnip field into a holiday camp in just one winter. They co-opted Billy Butlin into the Ministry of Supply.

Hore-Belisha, the man mostly remembered for installing the yellow flashing lights, 'Belisha Beacons,' at the edge of zebra crossings, was the Minister for War at the time. He put Butlin's holiday camp building experience to use by tasking him with building hutted camps for the army. The government at this point were still building camps based on plans from the Boer War. This worked out at a cost of £125 per hut. Butlin revised these plans and built them for £75 per hut. He built the army camps the government needed and made an agreement to buy them back, after the war, at three-fifths of the original cost, irrespective of the condition they were in. A risky strategy but one which was to pay off. Just two years after hostilities ceased, he had four holiday camps: Skegness, Filey, Clacton, and Pwllheli in Wales operating at full capacity.

A VERY DIFFERENT KIND OF opportunity came Billy Butlin's way in 1956. This time, not in the guise of government legislation, but on four legs in the form of 'Big Charlie', the largest elephant in captivity. As a story it might have been heaven sent for Butlin. The fate of 'Big Charlie', veteran of the Tarzan films, hung in the balance. He was no longer needed by the circus where he had been performing and his owner couldn't afford to keep him any longer. Some zoos expressed an interest in giving Charlie a home, but all these schemes foundered on the same problem: just how do you transport an Indian tusker, ten feet six inches tall, five feet wide and weighing in at around seven and a half ton from one end of the country to the other? If a new home couldn't be found for Big Charlie the only solution would be to shoot him. There was a public outcry.

Billy Butlin said he would be happy for Big Charlie to come and live at his Filey camp, but the problem remained of transporting this massive pachyderm from Butlin's Camp at Ayr in Scotland to Filey on the Yorkshire coast. This is where Butlin's flair for publicity kicked in. *He made it a competition.* He had learnt from years of judging knobbly knees,

72

beauty pageants and glamorous grandmother[2] contests that if you make a competition of something you are instantly onto a winner. He offered a £1,000 prize for anyone who could arrange safe transport for Charlie from Ayr to Butlin's Camp at Filey. Ideas for hair-brained elephant transportation schemes flooded in to Butlin's Oxford Street offices.

From the Nottingham College of Arts, 150 students proposed to tow Big Charlie around the coast on a raft. Another suggestion was of walking him along the seabed with his trunk attached to a giant snorkel. Some recommended using a tank landing craft; others favoured more of an airborne approach, such as constructing a giant net and suspending the elephant between two helicopters, or floating him along attached to a huge gas-filled balloon. None of these ideas were suitable, most were not even practical, but they generated a phenomenal amount of publicity for the holiday camp entrepreneur.

In practice it took four days to move Big Charlie. He had to be greased all over with margarine before he could be slipped into a custom-made, elephant-proof crate, built out of wooden railway sleepers, and fixed on a low loader. The move was masterminded, as Butlin had always intended, by Willie Wilson, Charlie's previous owner and a man with vast experience of transporting circus animals around the country. To add a bit of extra pizazz to the whole enterprise, Butlin arranged to have the Cornish wildlife expert Colonel 'Elephant' Bill Williams, a man who had spent most of his life working with elephants in the teak forests of Burma, ride shotgun.

Big Charlie was towed along the highway at a sedate three miles an hour on a route specially chosen to avoid low bridges and power cables. This being before the days of drink-driving laws and the breathalyser, the convoy would occasionally pull up at a pub along the way where one of the team would be despatched to the bar and order, 'seven double whiskies and fourteen buckets of water'. Big Charlie arrived at Filey to a huge ovation, which being an ex-circus elephant, he carried off with great aplomb and once established there he became a massive favourite with the children.

---

[2] Billy Butlin developed the idea for Glamorous Grandmother contests after a trip to the USA in 1955 when he met Marlene Dietrich, the star of films such as *The Blue Angel*, *Dishonoured*, and *Shanghai Express*. He was stunned to discover that someone so glamorous was also a grandmother.

A competition once again offered Billy Butlin the opportunity for national and international publicity when he took over the organisation and sponsorship of the annual Cross Channel Swim Competition in 1954, previously organised by the *Daily Mail*. Whilst this had the intended effect of raising the profile of Butlin's holiday camps it proved to be something of a poisoned chalice. Despite making his camps available to the international competitors for training and accommodation, he found himself on the receiving end of criticism one year when bad weather resulted in no finishers. If that wasn't bad enough, in 1956 he was called before the Foreign Office for a dressing down after he had summarily banned the Egyptian Team from the competition during the Suez Crisis.

After seven years he was glad to end his sponsorship of the Cross Channel Swim but it left a bit of a gap. Soon he was on the lookout for a new project. The still buoyant craze for marathon walking fitted the bill perfectly. The nation had been held in thrall as Dr Barbara Moore, living on her diet of fruit, nuts and honey, trudged doggedly down the country. If he was still undecided, the huge reception she received when she reached Land's End made up his mind. Riding this wave of publicity, he set about organising the 'walk to end all walks'; the first and the only footrace from John O'Groats to Land's End.

Chapter Nine: 'When the Gov'nor gets an idea ...'

BUTLIN'S OXFORD STREET TEAM APPEARED to take his sudden pronouncement in their stride. The prospect of putting all of their preparation work for the summer season on hold for a few weeks and throwing themselves into organising a walking or running race didn't seem to faze them in the least. Even if that race was from John O'Groats to Land's End, in the depths of winter and a race the like of which had never been attempted before. Their attitude was best summed up by one of their number who remarked, 'When the Gov'nor gets an idea nobody gets home.'

Butlin and his team's organisational abilities were phenomenal. Theirs was a 'can do' attitude. Every year they would feed, house and entertain more than 600,000 visitors in the Butlin's Holiday Camps. It was the same organisational mind-set which could turn a muddy turnip field into a fully-functioning holiday camp in the space of one short winter, organise a credible attempt at the Blériot London to Paris Air Race or even to transport a seven and a half ton elephant halfway across the country. They just heaved a collective sigh and simply got on with it.

Staff were taken away from normal duties of planning catering, accommodation and entertainment and put to the tasks of devising the route. They needed to organise marshalling and a system of check points. All of the Butlin's vehicles were freed up from their regular work and loaded with spades, blankets, thermos flasks and extra cans of petrol, ready to deal with the harsh weather conditions they expected to encounter in the far north of Scotland. An early expeditionary team was despatched, first to Wick and then on to John O'Groats, to plan the route, check out any available facilities, to book accommodation and make arrangements on the ground. In all, eighty Butlin vehicles and 132 regular staff were employed in organising and managing the race.

The route chosen for the Billy Butlin Walk closely followed the route used first by Sergeants Maloney and Evans, and more recently by Dr Barbara Moore.

From John O'Groats the walkers would head almost due south following the coast for a while. They would go past Keiss, skirting Sinclair Bay and on to Wick, the first town on the route. From Wick they would follow first the A99, then the A9, through Lybster, Dunbeath, Berridale and over the sea cliffs along the Ord of Caithness. From the Ord the road descended to Helmsdale where the first checkpoint at the Bridge Hotel would come as a relief.

Although the route had been hastily planned the Butlin team aimed to site each check point where the walkers and runners would have access to food, drink and shelter. Thirty-two checkpoints in all were planned and their locations varied from transport cafes, pubs, hotels, post offices and even an AA Box [3] at Johnston Bridge in Dumfries. Once the race itself was underway, some checkpoints were closed, some moved and, after a few racers began to cheat and take lifts, mobile or roving checkpoints were instigated.

Heading ever southwards from Helmsdale the route passed through Brora and Golspie, skirted Loch Fleet and along the Dornach Firth past Bonar Bridge, to the second checkpoint at the Lady Rose Hotel at Ardgay. The road bridge which now crosses the Firth between Dornach and Tain, and which would have saved walkers many weary miles, was not opened until 1991.

From Ardgay the competitors would race along the Cromarty Firth through Dingwall to the third checkpoint at the Lisiliand Guest House and then south to join Loch Ness and the Great Glen at Drumnadrochit.

The fourth checkpoint was at Grant's Garage in Fort Augustus, then participants would head out along Loch Oich and Loch Lochy to Fort

---

[3] In the era before mobile phones AA Boxes, a kind of telephone kiosk used by the Automobile Association, were a common sight on Britain's roads. The maximum number of AA boxes was 787 in 1968. Only nineteen still remain of which eight are Grade II listed.

William, under the shadow of Ben Nevis. The walkers would have another long detour at Ballachulish, the bridge there not being opened until 1975, and on to Glen Coe and the Kings House Hotel, the famous haunt of Scottish Climbers. After Glen Coe, there was no respite as they then were to cross the wild and featureless Rannoch Moor, before pressing south past the Bridge of Orchy and on to the seventh checkpoint at the post office in Crianlarich.

Bonny Banks or not, the walk avoided the more obvious southerly route along Loch Lomond, opting instead to head in a more easterly direction and then south to Callander and the eighth checkpoint at the Rex Café. After Callander the racers would head towards Stirling, Doune and Denny. Glasgow was bypassed to the east via Carluke, Lanark, Abington (the Valleyfield Transport Café and checkpoint eleven), Johnston Bridge (AA Box No. 708, check point twelve) and on to Fergusson's Transport Café for checkpoint thirteen at Kirkpatrick Fleming in Dumfries.

Butlin's racers would cross the border into England just south of Gretna Green, and press on to Penrith before the long slow climb up Shap, followed by the descent towards Kendal. This was the closest they would come to the English Lake District.

Slyne Road Garage, check point sixteen at Lancaster, was roughly the halfway point of the race; but there would be no time to linger as the route continued down the west side of the Pennines, through Lancashire, the Red Rose County, and on via Wigan and Warrington. There, the Horse and Jockey Hotel was checkpoint number eighteen.

By the time the walkers and runners had reached Whitchurch and Wellington, they were truly in the Midlands. Birmingham was bypassed to the west, via Kidderminster and Gloucester, as they headed for checkpoint twenty-four, the Railway Inn at Patchway, just north of Bristol. Once they were beyond Bristol and into the West Country they would surely be feeling they were on the homeward leg, but this would have been deceptive. There was still more than 120 miles to go, and some of the toughest walking in front of them, before Land's End.

Ben Jones at a checkpoint.

The route through the south-west peninsular was generally a few miles inland of the northern coast. They inevitably passed through Bridgwater. It is almost impossible to plan a route from John O'Groats to Land's End without passing through Bridgwater, where the River Parrett must be crossed. Beyond lay Waterloo Cross, Crediton, Tiverton, and Oakhampton on the edge of Dartmoor, where checkpoint twenty-eight was in the Sampford Bridge Tea House.

Beyond Oakhampton and Launceton lay yet another wild and exposed stretch of the route across Bodmin Moor. This would be like a sting in the tail for Butlin's now very weary trekkers. After Bodmin it was Indian Queens and Redruth for the penultimate checkpoint at the Mount Ambrose Inn, before the final dash past Sennen and on to the finish at Land's End.

ON THE 10TH FEBRUARY 1960, a mere five days after the newspaper headlines had been full of stories about the redoubtable Dr Barbara Moore reaching Land's End, marathon walking was once again in the news. This time it was a series of advertisements in all of the major newspapers promoting:

'The Butlin Walk
– John O'Groats to Land's End –
Mass start from John O'Groats February 27th at Dawn'.

THE START TIME WOULD LATER be brought forward to 5:00 pm on 26th February to get around the problem of finding overnight accommodation for more than 700 competitors at John O'Groats. The advert went on to offer substantial cash prizes: £1,000 for the first man and £1,000 for the first woman home, along with prizes for the runners up, and £100 for the oldest man, oldest woman, youngest boy and youngest girl to complete the route.

'Unless someone does something about it,' Billy Butlin was quoted as saying, 'the roads this summer will be cluttered with walkers trying to beat Dr Barbara Moore's record.'

Dr Moore herself was said to be 'interested' in the Billy Butlin Walk, but in the end she never applied to compete. During the early part of 1960 she was at the height of her popularity and was busy with other projects. Her (second) biography was being published in weekly excerpts in Sunday newspaper *The People*. She issued a writ against Associated Newspapers for what she believed had intimated that she had been commercially sponsored on her walk; and she issued a second writ against her neighbour, eighty-two year old Major-General Sir Kenneth Grey Buchanan regarding access to the forecourt in front of both of their homes. She was also busy planning a 3,200 mile walk from coast to coast across the USA which she was due to start in April.

Although Dr Barbara Moore did not take part in the Billy Butlin Walk, her presence cast a long shadow throughout. Every walker was well aware that if it hadn't been for her and her marathon walking exploits, there would not be a race and they would not be taking part. And more than a few of the participants, as they ploughed through horizontal sleet on Scotland's most wild and exposed roads, would heartily wish she had never come to England but had stayed in deepest Russia.

She had succeeded in one regard however, that of linking diet to marathon walking in the minds of the public. One of the questions all competitors were asked on the application form for the Butlin Walk was if they intended to eat a specific diet for the duration of the race. And a considerable number said they would stick to Dr Barbara's diet.

APPLICATIONS FLOODED IN TO BUTLIN'S Oxford Street offices and the Post Office had to lay on extra delivery vans to cope with the volume of mail. There were more than 4,000 applications, each of which needed to be sent an official application form by post. When these were returned the numbers of applicants were whittled down to 1,500 and this number was again reduced to 715 by the start of the race.

Competitors each received their race number to wear on their front and back. These were white with bold black numbers and made of a tough rubberised fabric with a hole at each corner so the walker could tie them in place with string or tape. The one to be worn on the back also had a small red reflector fixed to it as a safety measure. Billy Butlin wore number thirteen even though it was clear from the records that number thirteen had originally been allocated to James Nicol, a thirty-seven year old walker from Airdrie in Lanarkshire. On the list of competitors his name had been circled with the letters W.E.B. (William Edmund Butlin) jotted next to it. So Mr Holiday Camps himself wore number thirteen and an unsuspecting James Nicol had to content himself with number 1,244.

Billy Butlin (centre) wearing race number 13 in the early stages of the race.

Along with their race number, competitors also received their race card with their photo attached, which they exchanged for a check and identity book before the start. The check book was dark blue with gold lettering, with the outline of Great Britain on the cover. It was like a small passport with the competitor's photo inside and spaces for it to be stamped at each of the thirty-two checkpoints along the route. On the page facing the photo, Billy Butlin had written a stirring message to all competitors.

'This is a tough assignment and you will be called upon to show courage and endurance of the highest order.

The pages of this book represent a permanent record of your response to this great challenge.

Good luck.'

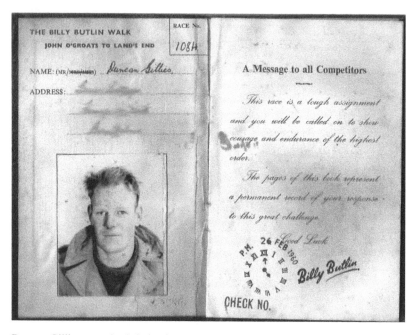

Duncan Gillies race check-in book.

IF THIS MESSAGE WASN'T SUFFICIENT, it was accompanied by a letter setting out in no uncertain terms just how challenging the race would be and stressing how it was up to the competitor to be self-reliant.

'…Arrangements for resting and feeding en route are, as you know, your own responsibility… The race is a tough venture and your endurance test …local amenities could not possibly cater for everyone …'

EVEN THOUGH ALL COMPETITORS SIGNED and returned a postcard to say that they understood exactly the nature of the expedition they were taking on, as soon as the race started Butlin would find himself the target of criticism from the press, the police, members of parliament local government officials and even the racers themselves for the rigors they were exposed to.

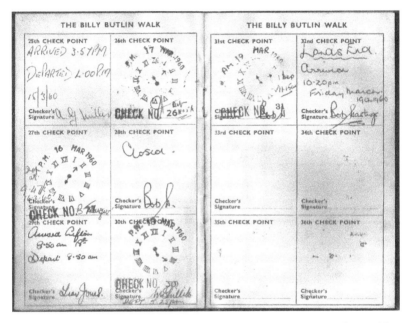

Final page of Duncan Gillies's check-in book with Land's End entry. After reaching Land's End he walked back to London.

REX NORTH, IN HIS BIOGRAPHY of Billy Butlin written just two years after the big walk, highlights three reasons why a John O'Groats to Land's End race seemed such a winner to Butlin. Firstly, the Cross Channel Swim had been well established as an annual event by this time and whilst it generated publicity when it began, its novelty value had diminished considerably. Secondly, it being the depths of winter, the camps were idle and an event such as the Butlin Race would raise the profile of his holiday business at a time of year when holidays were not uppermost in the publics' minds. Finally, North suggested that Butlin had recognised how marathon treks had quickly become a national craze

and by catching the mood of the nation he could see tremendous scope
for organising a major race walk.

Duncan Gillies's race number.

IF A FOOT RACE WAS to be planned across the length of Britain for more
than 700 competitors, most of whom had little or no experience of
walking in extreme conditions, a start in the last few days of February in
the far north of Caithness, a place not renowned for its balmy winters,
would seem to be just about as crazy as it is possible to be. Yet this is
exactly what Billy Butlin was organising. If the wild weather and isolated
location were two factors against the walk there were two equally strong
reasons for the walk. Firstly, Butlin was catching the mood of the nation
which was still fired-up and enthusiastic about Dr Moore's epic trek. If
he had left it until the spring when the weather was likely to be kinder,
the public may well have gone off the idea. Marathon walking was a

craze and crazes tend to only have a short lifespan. Also in the depths of winter he could commit all his resources to the race and still have time to get his holiday camps ready. He wouldn't be able to do this if all of his staff were busy running his camps during the summer season.

Billy Butlin made it clear that he saw this race as a race for the people, the ordinary man or woman in the street. 'Long-distance walking,' he said, 'was something ordinary people felt *they* could do.' The wealthy and the very skilled may have specialist sports like horse racing or mountaineering yet any regular person, with a reasonable amount of fitness could walk. And they did. The British public loved him for it and they signed up for his race in their hundreds.

IF THE WALK WAS PROVING a big hit with the public at large it did not go down anything like as well with the Scottish authorities. 'Outrageous!' thundered Sir Myer Gaipern, the Lord Provost of Glasgow, in *The Times*. He accused Billy Butlin of turning Dr Barbara Moore's walk into '…the biggest advertising stunt of the century.' The Chief Constable of Caithness, Mr John Georgeson was no more complimentary. He declared the walk to be 'ill-timed', and cited the freezing temperatures and lack of any form of shelter in the early part of the route. The Sutherland County Council's finance committee took the decision to oppose the race, its chairman George McIver stating, 'I have absolutely no doubt that if 300 people were trapped on one stretch there could be the chance of 50 to 100 of them dying … Some might not last half an hour.'

Butlin remained quite unmoved by these very public tirades. He was well used to being on the receiving end of stiff opposition. Every holiday camp he had ever built was initially met with strong opposition from local people, county councillors and especially from shopkeepers who would always complain that it would ruin their business. In practice the building of a holiday camp invariably meant jobs, increased prosperity, and more money coming into the local economy, just as the arrival of hundreds of walkers and runners to Caithness would be good for local coffers. Butlin's cause wasn't helped by a deterioration in the weather, as the start of the race drew near and a big freeze set in.

As the snow fell and the mercury plummeted, the roads around John O'Groats became blocked and impassable. When snowploughs could get through, they heaped snow and ice in great mounds at the side of the roads. Particularly badly affected was the road over the Ord of Caithness, an exposed and windswept cliff 600 feet above the sea just north of Helmsdale, and the walk's first checkpoint. Once considered to be the most dangerous stretch of road in Scotland, the Ord was an unavoidable part of the route early in the race.

Two days before the start of the race the freezing weather dealt yet another a blow to Butlin's preparations when a Land Rover carrying Clem Cummings, described as Butlin's 'chief organiser' skidded on a frozen road at Ardgay near Bonar Bridge and plunged fifteen feet down an embankment. Clem and his two travelling companions were taken to Hospital at Golspie and while their injuries were not considered serious, they were kept in for a few days, forcing race marshal Sam Rockett to hastily reorganise his stewarding and checkpoint teams.

Despite external pressure, road traffic accidents and the prophecies of doom, Billy Butlin himself remained bullish. 'Let the people march,' he told the press. 'My marathon trek goes on ... I'll carry the can, [and accept] total responsibility for anything that goes wrong.'

Questions were being asked in the House of Commons and an appeal was sent to the Right Honourable Mr John Scott Maclay, the Secretary of State for Scotland, asking him to intervene and stop the race. Still Billy Butlin held firm.

It would be fair to say that the press corps themselves were anything but happy about the Butlin Race and there is no doubt this was reflected in their reporting. They were not so much unhappy about the race itself, or the plight of the hapless competitors battling the Scottish weather, but rather at the prospect of being dragged away from the comforts of Fleet Street in the depths of winter to cover a race in snow-bound Scotland. They were doubly upset when they arrived in Wick and John O'Groats to discover that what little accommodation there was had been booked solid by Butlin's staff or race competitors who'd arrived early. So the reporters of the nation's major newspapers were reduced to sleeping in draughty corridors and even on billiard tables. Calling it off would have been an even bigger news story than the race going ahead but Billy Butlin failed to oblige and they had to content themselves with the prospect of two to three weeks out in the very worst of weathers covering Butlin's mammoth trek.

For all the media reports, the tub-thumping and grandstanding from politicians, nobody in the Butlin's organisation had actually received any official communication from the Secretary of State for Scotland asking them to postpone the race. Commenting on this pre-race crisis after the event, Billy Butlin outlined how seriously he took his obligation to the contestants. 'It was a great responsibility, so we took great precautions … When the weather was bad two days before it started, there were 700 people all over Britain making their way to Scotland, I couldn't just call it off and leave them stranded.' He went on to explain how he booked two big halls in Wick where they could be fed and looked after until conditions improved and that he had arranged for eight helicopters to be on standby if any needed rescuing.

Not everyone in officialdom was opposed to the walk however. Eighty-five year old Mr G Abrich McKay, a Caithness County Councillor argued, 'It will do more to boost Caithness than anything before.' And he offered to walk the first fifty yards with Mr Butlin.

The local people had mixed feelings about the walk. Most were surprised and rather pleased to find their sleepy little community the focus of such a high profile national event. Some were less keen, as *The Times* quoted after they had interviewed one of John O'Groats more dour residents. 'We have a word for it in Scotland,' he said, 'daft.'

Billy Butlin countered all the criticism by pointing out that he would have fifty vans patrolling the route to help any walkers in distress and said that he would walk the first fifty miles himself, which he considered to be the most demanding in terms of weather conditions. This was a promise he would later regret. On 24th February the Right Honourable Mr John Scott Maclay, the Secretary of State for Scotland, decided he had no power to intervene in the walk and on Thursday 25th February *The Times* stated that the 'BUTLIN RACE WILL START AS PLANNED.'

Chapter Ten: The Yukon

BY THE 25TH FEBRUARY THE weather had begun to relent. A thaw had set in and conditions slowly began to improve. Snow was still heaped along the verges but the roads themselves were passable with care, the Ord of Caithness being an exception. Up there, vehicles still had to be hauled through by snowploughs.

John O'Groats was a village under siege. For those few days in the depths of winter in 1960 when the Billy Butlin Race hit town it was more like a Gold Rush boomtown or, as *The Daily Sketch* said, it was 'Like the Yukon.' Tents and marquees had sprung up, transforming a normally sleepy village into a new, if very temporary, metropolis and focus of the nation's media. Never before, nor since for that matter, had John O'Groats ever seen a gathering quite like the start of the Billy Butlin Race.

The village of John O'Groats, in 1960, was not vastly different from how it looks today. 'Nothing there but a stick and a hotel,' said one local taxi driver. There is a tiny port with a stone pier, a hotel, a shop or two, a scattering of houses, and the famous signpost, pointing to Land's End 874 miles away. It is a small community at the busiest of times. Just a handful of travellers arrive to take the ferry over to the Orkney Islands; a few visitors are drawn there because it is the most north-easterly village on the mainland and the starting or the finishing point for walkers or cyclists trekking to or from Land's End. Purists might point out that Duncansby Head, two miles beyond John O'Groats is, strictly speaking, the most north-easterly point and many End to Enders, the author included, choose to start or end their walk there.

The Butlin team erected three huge marquees; one for the competitors to check in and be given their race numbers and logbook, one for refreshments, and one which was largely annexed by the press corps. The hotel was decked with bunting and race banners and the narrow roads were jammed with buses, cars, TV trucks, and lots of yellow and blue Butlin's vans. The air vibrated with activity as hundreds of competitors arrived, checked in and then tried to find somewhere to rest amongst the press of bodies as race officials dashed around making last minute arrangements. Over the whole proceedings was the clatter of the Butlin's helicopter as it swooped and hovered over the start.

DESPITE HAVING A ROUGH TIME of it in terms of their accommodation, the press had a field day. Here was a great news event, in the depths of winter a few weeks after Christmas and the New Year, usually a pretty thin time for news. As a story it had all the elements they could wish for: the people's hero in conflict with the authorities over whether the race should go ahead or not. The threat of disaster and more than a hint of danger in the air, at least if nay-saying officials were to be believed. Just a day before the race was due to start, the *Daily Mirror* were still referring to it as the 'Death Trek.' And there was Billy Butlin himself, with his flair for publicity and an instinct for what the person on the street wanted. He was always good for copy. The press sensed there were a few more rounds to play out in that particular battle and they wanted to make sure they had ringside seats.

Before the off most TV and newspaper reporters filled their time by interviewing race competitors, asking them why they were putting their lives on hold for two or three weeks and setting out to race the length of Scotland and England. Most said they were attracted by the big cash prizes. The £1,000 cheque for the winner was a huge amount of money in 1960 when the average weekly wage was just a little over £14. Twenty-six year old Oswald Balwant Singh from London said he wanted to win the money to pay for his education. David Doran from Wigan also had learning in mind. He said he'd use the money to send his son to college. Frederick Gaplen from Wimbledon saw the race as 'a challenge to fate' and needed the money to help care for his wife and son, who both suffered from Polio. Many said that they were entering for the challenge, to test themselves; some said how they had been inspired by Dr Barbara Moore and wanted to see how they could do.

Competitors came from every walk of life and their marathon walking credentials were every bit as varied. Brothers Hamish and Kenneth Mackay from Conon-Bridge, Rosshire, both footballers with Ross County FC, were two of the many sportsmen who entered. Hector Bonallo, from Southport in Lancashire, had played for the English International Baseball Team, and eighteen year old Michael Day from London had captained his school football team. Twenty year old John Christopher Andrews, from Yeovil in Somerset, was a motorcycle scramble rider and was up for anything 'with a tinge of danger in it.' Many of the contestants were or had been boxers, at either a professional or an amateur level, including Ric Sanders, John Henry Kent, Clarence Harold Barker and thirty-nine year old John Conroy, the ex-professional from Roxburghshire.

The armed forces were well represented as they had been all the way through the marathon walking craze. There were two military policemen, Peter Topham and James Maitland, both twenty-two and based at the Redford Barracks in Edinburgh, and Frederick John Allan, a retired RAF Squadron Leader from Bitterne Park Southampton. Keith Dreamer Banwell, forty-two from Potter's Bar in Middlesex had competed in the farcical *News of the World* 'March of the Century', and John Sinclair, also forty-two from Leicester, had been one of the joint winners.

A goodly number of entrants came from the world of the performing arts. Twenty-seven year old Madeleine Inwood from Bedfordshire was a Bluebell Girl and circus performer. Tony Parr from Barnet in Hertfordshire was the leader of a jazz band, Barry Thornton from Sheffield described himself as a pop singer and Albert Eadie from Kilmarnock was the leader of the 'Harmonikords'. Forty-five year old P. Singh had worked on the film *Sabu* and Dennis William Sturgess from Chatham in Kent had appeared in the classic 1957 David Lean film *Bridge Over the River Kwai*, along with having climbed Mount Kilimanjaro.

Then there was a plethora of human interest stories, people like fifty year old Mrs Ivy Bayliss from West Bromwich in the Midlands. Ivy just enjoyed walking. She would never catch a bus if she could walk and every week she'd walk from Greets Green over to Dudley to see her sister and then walk all the way back again. Her workmates at the Dart Spring Company said that a walker like her should go in for it, so she took their advice, and entered.

There was a strong contingent of entrants who had done well in other recent marathon walks. Wilfred Cowley won the London to Brighton Race. Dorothy Jonnone from Whitstable in Kent had walked Edinburgh to Marble Arch in just six days the previous month, and Wilfred Woodford, twenty-six from Bognor Regis, had won the Pagham Pram Race for the last two years.

Then there were those who undoubtedly added colour to the overall picture but whose qualifications were at best questionable, such as thirty year old Mark Henry White from Carterton in Oxford who listed his hobbies as Spanish dancing and Bull-fighting. John Fryer, twenty-six from Acton in London, claimed to 'prefer walking to working'. Other entrants were Vera Wright, the first woman to descend the deepest pothole in the world, and fifty year old Mrs Davina Landells from Edinburgh, better known to her friends as 'Dauntless Dav'. Betty St Ledger, from Gerrards Cross, had spent fifteen years in China, William Francis Thomas was a member of the Health and Strength League and Sydney Mitchell from Mansfield was a bus conductor.

Victor G.V. Norwood from Scunthorpe seemed to have led an interesting life. He had been a member of expeditions to Guiana and Brazil and described himself as an amateur boxing champion, a professional wrestler and former concert singer who was now trying his hand at being an author. He was in fact a prolific pulp fiction writer with a string of Westerns and Crime Thrillers to his name. In the section on his dietary requirements, he specified that he would live on just one meal per day.

David A. Wathen, thirty-one from Selkirk and who described himself as a 'hill sheep farmer,' was also an author. He had edited and published the book *Harehunters All* in 1951 and even though he failed to complete the whole walk he would go on to write the official account of the Billy Butlin race, *The Big Walk*, under the rather unconvincing pseudonym of 'A. Walker'. In answer to the question of diet he said he was tempted to write in something facetious such as 'goat's eyes and fried legs of ptarmigan', but instead listed normal, wholesome and sustaining food.

Yeolanda Sutherland from Ashford in Kent said she intended to follow Dr Moore's diet as did Om Prakash Magoon from Doncaster. Custan Eugene Travers from Bingley was sticking to a vegetarian diet as was forty year old Ron Thomson from Andover and twenty-seven year old Sylvia Gourlay from London. Gary MacDonell from London was planning to eat nothing, and only drink milk all the way while sixty-five year old Jim Spence from Glasgow would drink a pint of liquid per day. Charles William Chivers, who was 'strongly against all forms of sport' would eat no hot meals, Miss Lavenia Whippy would drink Ovaltine, while Miss Frances Penman from Kirkintilloch would have a switched egg every third day. Chris Koch, an ex-rugby player from Perranporth in Cornwall was convinced that lots of fresh fruit and All-Bran would keep him going. Richard Cosgrove, a student nurse from Liverpool was keeping his diet a secret while Keith Simpson from Hebden Bridge didn't mind who knew that he was planning to sustain himself on 'Fat meat or bacon, raw veg, fruit and stale bread.'

The most popular diets were based on steak, suet, honey, eggs and milk supplemented by plenty of Mars bars. In practice most walkers couldn't carry much food with them and, other than those who had brought their own support team along to look after their food and accommodation, they had to live on whatever they could get along the way from cafes, shops and hotels.

THE COMPETITORS GATHERING AT JOHN O'Groats could be divided broadly into three categories. There were the contenders: serious athletes, men and women who trained and regularly competed in athletic events, race walkers, marathon runners and distance racers. The best organised of these were accompanied by a support team who would follow the runner with a caravan or campervan so they could make sure their competitor was supplied with food and drink and always had somewhere to rest. Some members of the team would also act as pacemakers trotting along in front of the runner to make sure they put in the best possible performance.

Many of the regular competitors thought these 'professional' athletes with their trainers and support teams had an unfair advantage and that it was not in keeping with the spirit of the race as an event for the people. This seems a fair point. Racers with support teams were not slowed down by having to carry their gear, nor did they waste time and energy finding somewhere to sleep each night. There was talk about having entry classes for supported and unsupported competitors the following year.

The second group of competitors were the fit and well organised, racers who expected to complete the course, put in good time and have a shot at the prize money. These were people competing in the spirit of Dr Barbara Moore's treks and the new marathon walking craze. It wouldn't be stretching a point to say that these sporting and adventurous types were really the backbone of the event. The sort of people Billy Butlin had in mind when he organised the race. These were the 'have-a-go' types who, with a bit of grit and determination, could, and did, achieve great things.

The third group competing in the Great Butlin Walk were the eccentrics. They may have had no chance of winning, probably little chance of even completing the course but the race would have been the poorer without them. One such person was the fifty-seven year old New York lawyer wearing a conical Chinese farmer's hat, held in place with string, a transparent British war gas cape and plimsolls on his feet, who would tell anyone who would listen his theories of correlation while pouring scorn on 'that imposter' Einstein and his theories of relativity. He did not officially join the race however, claiming that, 'As an American citizen it is beneath my dignity to take part in the race for money.'

Some competitors didn't have a clue where John O'Groats was, or indeed where Land's End was in relation to it. David Wathen (A. Walker) reported a story about a man from Liverpool who hopped on a northbound bus from Glasgow, handed the female conductor half a crown (twelve and a half pence) and asked to be put off at John O'Groats. After the start some walkers had barely covered twenty miles before they were asking Butlin if they were there yet.

RACE COMPETITORS CAME FROM EVERY walk of life. Twenty were over pensionable age, one had a wooden leg and two were blind. The nobility was represented in the form of sixty-eight year old Edward Fitzgerald, the Duke of Leinster. With his sporting and adventurous reputation, a hike from John O'Groats to Land's End might seem like something of a breeze. He once made a sea trip right around the coast of Britain in a twelve foot canoe and on another occasion he won a bet of £3,000 by driving from London to Aberdeen in less than fifteen hours. Sadly he fell foul of the regulations early in the race when he took a lift and was disqualified. He appealed arguing that he just took the lift to his overnight rest stop when he was exhausted and he re-joined the race from the exact same spot the next morning. After an enquiry by race marshal Sam Rockett, he was reinstated.

If twenty-one year old Philip Barker from Hampstead, wearing race number 575, wasn't nobility he certainly dressed the part. With his bowler hat, tightly furled umbrella, dark jacket and striped trousers, regulation dress for bankers in the City of London in the 1960s, he seemed impervious to the Scottish weather. A pair of gym shoes were his only concession to the walk. His support team following in a camper van carried all fourteen of his city suits for him. On Sundays he would wear a morning suit and a grey top hat.

One of the most popular competitors with both the public and other racers was tiny forty-four year old Miss Lavenia Whippy, originally from Fiji but by then living in London, who walked in bare feet. Her beaming smile and sunny disposition won over everyone's hearts. She could be seen stepping briskly out wearing a bright blue tracksuit and carrying a parasol. Seventy-two year old Mr William Tully, who was totally deaf and unable to hear the traffic, wore a miner's lamp on his head so that passing cars could see him at night.

Walkers chose an elaborate and eclectic mix of gear. Ex-army clothing was plentiful and could be bought quite cheaply from Army Surplus stores, and as many of the competitors had been in the forces, battledress, military boots, and ammo pouches for stowing gear were popular. Many carried small rucksacks and kit was often a combination of hiking and running gear. Some wore tracksuits, some plus fours and, as they were in Scotland, some even wore kilts. Footwear was just as varied; hiking boots, sandals, plimsolls, baseball boots and in one case Wellington boots. Forty-six year old Ben Jones from Swansea worked as a linesman for the Central Electricity Generating Board and would walk twenty-five to thirty miles each day following the powerlines over hills, dales, through hedges and streams wearing Wellington boots. So naturally, and much to the amazement of his fellow walkers, he planned to wear his wellies all the way to Land's End.

Ben (the boots) Jones walked the entire route in a pair of Wellington boots. He came fifth.

As START TIME APPROACHED, THE huddled masses of competitors began to organise themselves. There was an initial chaotic practice start, an hour before the official off, when some competitors went cantering down the road thinking the race had actually begun. Finally all 715 racers were gathered together and herded towards the start, creating a press of bodies, shoulder to shoulder, all keen to begin. Some competitors edged to the front aiming for a fast get-away hoping it would give them an advantage. Some were happy to be further back to avoid the inevitable initial surge and believing that the pack would sort itself out over the first few miles.

So on Friday 26th February 1960, a mere twenty-two days after Dr Barbara Moore had reached Land's End, at 5pm on a bright clear evening Billy Butlin fired a Very pistol into the air to start the first and only Butlin's John O'Groats to Land's End Race. Twelve red and green rockets arced up into the night sky and the Wick Girl Pipers played "Scotland the Brave" as, in a never to be repeated spectacle, the competitors surged down the narrow road, the leaders running like greyhounds released from the traps, all intent on being the first to reach Land's End almost 900 miles away.

The mass start with the John O'Groats Hotel in the background.

Chapter Eleven: Scooped

FOR THOSE FIRST FEW PRECIOUS minutes, as the runners galloped away from the start, twenty year old D.A. Nelson, proudly wearing number 501 on his chest, was the race leader. He was hotly pursued by number 317 W.L. Fraser, aged thirty-one who was in turn being chased by forty year old J.D. Wood wearing number 194. Then the chasing pack caught up and they began to slip down the field.

The brutal weather in the run up to the race had eased and on that first night it was a clear, cold evening as the competitors bobbed and jogged their way along the gently inclined road which ran south from John O'Groats. Over the first few miles, and after the initial rush had spent itself, the racers began to sort themselves out into some sort of order. Fit and serious competitors moved towards the front of the pack and began to dispute the lead as the slower runners, the walkers, the not-so-fit, and the no-hopers began to fall behind.

Billy Butlin himself, wearing a white fur hat any Cossack would have been proud of, a duffle coat and race number thirteen, was striding out with the best of them. By his own admission he was not particularly fit, yet he set out to walk the first fifty miles of the race to make good on a promise given, a little rashly perhaps, when he was being hounded by the press and officials to call off the race. He had told them that he did not see any danger in the race, that the first fifty miles would be the worst because of the weather, and that he would walk that himself, 'Even if it kills me!' He later estimated that he'd walked 100 miles of the route overall, organising and patrolling back and forth. Tramping the first fifty miles was proving something of a problem for Butlin, not so much because of his lack of fitness, but because it kept him from being able to oversee this crucial early part of the race. In the end he climbed into a car after just five miles and then walked and rode alternatively through the night until 2:30 in the morning when his car became stuck behind a broken-down vehicle just north of the first race checkpoint at Helmsdale.

For the first part of the night the weather was fair, even mild for the time of year with just a light breeze, but in the early hours a weather front swept in bringing wind, icy rain and hail. By the time the racers had reached Keiss, a small village twelve miles out, a good deal of them were starting to wonder what they'd let themselves in for and even more began to regret the mad charge at start of the race, when they had set themselves too fast a pace.

When they reached Wick, another ten miles further along, the number of bodies falling by the wayside were mounting as competitors in their droves dropped out of the race. Many who had entered the Butlin Race had been swept along by a wave of enthusiasm for marathon walking and perhaps a little bit of Dr Barbara Moore's reflected glory, never thinking seriously about their own level of fitness, the weather conditions or the sort of commitment a trek on this scale would entail.

The problem of walkers overestimating their level of fitness quickly became critical as the number of dropouts increased. Next morning the *Daily Mirror* were reporting, '150 LIMP OUT OF THE GREAT MARCH – Less than five hours and seventeen miles from the start – 30 (all MEN) in hospital'.

This huge and unexpected early dropout rate presented an immediate problem to race organisers and they responded as best they could. A local seamen's mission in Wick was opened to provide them with shelter and somewhere to rest and the two tiny local hospitals were quickly swamped and had to send out an urgent call for extra staff. The police opened the doors of the town's jail and exhausted, soaking wet walkers were crammed in five to a cell. All of the early dropouts were exhausted, hungry, and a few required minor medical treatment. A substantial number claimed they were destitute and had no funds to pay their way back home.

As is often the case in a situation like this the finger of blame was quickly pointed at Billy Butlin. The organisers naturally had an obligation to their competitors but this did not absolve the walkers' responsibility for themselves and Butlin had made it quite clear throughout, and in their letter of acceptance, that competitors were expected to be self-reliant and to fend for themselves. The unexpected tsunami of early exhausted, penniless dropouts provided opponents of the race yet more ammunition to criticise Butlin. When it was revealed that destitute competitors were going into police stations and the Town Hall to ask for 'National Assistance', a form of state aid of the time, and their fare home, the *Guardian* ran the headline; 'WEARY WALKERS WANT CASH - Assistance Board rejects claims'.

The Butlin's organisation was forced to respond to this unexpected, and as it turned out costly, set of new demands. The hungry were fed and the weary were given somewhere to rest and those requiring treatment were patched up. Nobody suffered from anything much worse than blisters or muscle strain, and in the end Billy Butlin paid all the hospital bills himself. Those who had no money (or at least said they had no money) were bought a ticket home and put on a train. The railway had to put another carriage on the southbound train to cope with all the unexpected race dropouts. Billy Butlin estimated later that he had paid out several thousand pounds to bail out the apparently destitute competitors who had dropped out early and he told a *Guardian* reporter that next year he would check that every competitor had enough cash with them to be able to pay their fare back home.

The start time of the race had been brought forward from the original plan of setting off at dawn on Saturday 27th February to five pm on the Friday evening to relieve the pressure of having to find somewhere for all 715 competitors to sleep at John O'Groats where, quite simply, there were nothing like enough beds. For all of his preparations, the cash outlay, the controversy as to whether the race should have been called off or not, and the undoubted newsworthiness of the story, Billy Butlin must have hoped that his race would dominate the newspaper headlines on the Saturday morning. But he was to be disappointed. He was scooped by the highest authority in the land, the royal family.

As Butlin's racers were jogging down the road from John O'Groats only one hour and fifteen minutes into the race, a Court Circular was issued from Clarence House announcing that Princess Margaret, the Queen's younger sister, was to marry Mr Anthony Armstrong-Jones.

This announcement came quite out of the blue and took the press totally by surprise. Princess Margaret, who only a few years earlier had been embroiled in constitutional controversy when she wanted to marry divorcee Group Captain Peter Townsend (her father King George VI's former equerry), was to marry a commoner, the photographer Anthony Armstrong-Jones. The Billy Butlin Race was instantly relegated from the front page to page three.

If Wick was the place where the problem of early dropouts came to its head, most competitors remembered the little town for the rousing welcome the locals gave them. Spectators lined the streets and cheered themselves hoarse as each of the walkers passed through. Such was the local enthusiasm that a number of tired, dispirited racers who were on the brink of giving up, were re-energised by the warmth and enthusiasm of the crowd and kept going instead. This welcome proved the lie that the press were spinning. They had said how the local people of the far north of Scotland didn't want the event and would like to have seen it cancelled. Nothing could have been further from the truth. Quite apart from the attention and prestige it brought to this oft forgotten corner of Scotland, it was a boon to the local economy. Cafés, pubs and hotels were all besieged with customers. The hotel at Lybster was churning out cooked breakfasts at a phenomenal rate and only stopped when they ran out of food.

The local people in the north of Scotland took the competition to their hearts and as an area long renowned for warmth and hospitality, so it was proved when the Great Billy Butlin Race passed through. Farms, houses, and crofters all opened their doors to walkers. They took them in, fed them, dried their wet clothes and gave them somewhere to sleep, and in most cases they refused any form of payment at all. Ben Jones, the man from Swansea walking in his Wellington boots, was trudging on past Latheronwheel at three o'clock on Saturday morning, soaked through by the rain when a local man came out of his house and took him in. He and his wife cooked Ben a meal, hung his wet clothes up to dry, gave him a bed for the night (warmed with hot water bottles) and cooked him breakfast next morning before they sent him on his way. As his clothes were still not dry they insisted he borrow some of their son's clothes and they posted his own clothes on to Gretna for him to pick up later. And they wouldn't accept any payment at all.

The extreme winter weather which had threatened the start of the race had not yet relinquished its icy grip. The Ord of Caithness between Berriedale and Helmsdale had been cleared, but huge piles of snow and ice were still banked on either side of the road, obscuring any view other than the road in front or the stars above. Some walkers made their crossing in the dark ricocheting off the frozen walls on each side of the road like pinballs. Conditions underfoot were little better. Packed ice and granite chips would suddenly give way to bare tarmac six inches below, causing the walkers to stumble on the uneven surface. In the dark, ridges of ice and boulders were only discovered by barked shins and grazed knees. In the energy-sapping cold the walkers were relieved when the A9 began its long slow descent and the lights of Helmsdale could be seen winking in the distance.

The race leader, even at this early stage, was twenty-six year old John Grundy, wearing race number 127, a lorry driver from Wakefield in West Yorkshire. Standing at just five foot three inches tall some newspapers likened him to a racing whippet. His running style was said to be effortless with 'piston-like legs pounding over the road.' On his application form he described himself as a 'first-class road runner and second class marathon runner (AAA)'. He intended to run all the way and would be in the lead for much of the race. Grundy was a committed runner. He even blamed his love of running for the break-up of his marriage. In the past, or so he told the *Daily Mail*, he had been just a little too fond of having a pint or two out with the lads. His wife objected to this and suggested he take up some sport instead. So he took up running and became so keen he spent his every evening out training. Initially his wife would follow him to athletic events but in the end she had just had enough. He may have lost a wife, but he became the favourite for the men's race even if the Amateur Athletics Association took away his amateur status.

Grundy covered the first twenty miles in a sprightly two hours and twenty minutes, then he pressed on to Dunbeath thirty-nine miles from the start where he stopped to rest for what was left of the night. Richard Penman, a distillery worker from Glasgow and member of Bellahouston Harriers was following in second place.

John Grundy (127) and pacemaker on the road.

For the frontrunners, in both the men's and women's races a pattern quickly began to emerge, a pattern which would become the story of the race as they progressed through Britain. The race leader would surge ahead, often putting in a phenomenal performance and covering a vast distance very quickly only to be overtaken when they finally had to stop to take a rest. David Robinson took the lead from John Grundy at Dunbeath, but unlike John Grundy, David Robinson just didn't stop.

Bearded David Robinson, who prompted the *Daily Mail* headline, 'The Beard Still Leads' on the 29th of February, was a thirty-five year old graduate research student from the London School of Economics, who hailed originally from Bermuda. He attracted a massive amount of popularity by being the only serious contender amongst the early leaders who had no support team. He wore German training shoes, and a tracksuit made of the same waterproof fabric as Sir Edmund Hillary and Sherpa Tenzing had worn when they summited Mount Everest seven years earlier. He stormed ahead covering his first 100 miles in twenty-three hours. He paused briefly at Golspie to buy a present for his wife, which he handed to *Empire News* reporter Liam Regan to post home, then he pressed on. By the time he reached Drumnadrochit on Loch Ness he was averaging seventy-three miles a day. His race strategy was to walk up hills and run the downhill and flat sections. He was able to maintain his lead as far as Fort William, but when he stopped briefly for a meal and a rest John Grundy took the lead from him.

The issue of whether competitors should run or only walk was something of a hot topic. Some purists argued that the race was billed as a walk so running should be outlawed. Hungarian born Alfred Rozentals, a miner living in Bilsthorpe Nottinghamshire, took a firm line on this matter. He insisted he would only walk and would not run even an inch. He believed that if he walked and didn't burn himself out running he would, like the tortoise and the hare, be able to maintain a fast walking pace far longer than the runners would be able to keep going. There was clearly some merit in this approach; he was in the leading group throughout the race and took over the lead from John Grundy at Crianlarich.

Billy Butlin (centre) with Wendy Lewis (right) and Beryl Randle (left) at Land's End.

His refusal to run was perhaps a little pedantic. Although the race was styled as 'The Butlin Walk' in the original advert, the rules did not specify that competitors could only walk. Butlin offered competitors rather more scope – 'walk, run, skip or jump' – he'd said, the winner would be 'the fastest time, unaided, on their own two feet'.

In the women's race there were only ever two serious contenders. Thirty-one year old Beryl Randle, wearing race number 205, a secretary from Walsall in the Midlands, had cited her achievements somewhat modestly on her application as the, 'four-time winner of the British one mile track walk'. Tom Morris, in his account *The Long Walk*, describes Beryl Randle as a road walking 'superstar ... even in the days before the term had been invented'. Striding out from John O'Groats dressed in a navy blue donkey jacket, grey trousers, leather walking shoes and with a green woolly hat on her head, there were no women's road walking accolades she hadn't won. She was the queen of British race walking and like John Grundy she would lose her amateur status by entering the Butlin Race.

The young pretender for Beryl's crown was eighteen year old Wendy Lewis from Liverpool, wearing race number 662 and weighing in at a mere eight stone. This was the same Wendy Lewis who had just completed a John O'Groats to Land's End walk in twenty-three days, finishing on 7th February, only days after Dr Moore. Wendy took barely three weeks to recover before heading back to John O'Groats, ready to walk the whole distance once more. This time instead of walking, her older sister Joy was driving a car as part of her support team. Slim dark-haired Wendy, dressed in a scarlet anorak, tartan trousers, white plimsolls and with her lipstick matching her jacket, skipped over the ground at a gentle jogging pace. She quickly became the poster girl of the Billy Butlin Race.

Chapter Twelve: On the Road

AS THE RACERS MADE THEIR way along the shores of Loch Ness and passed the village of Drumnadrochit, David Robinson was in the lead with Glasgow's Richard Penman second and John Grundy in third place. Quite unknown to the leaders at that point was just how the number of competitors in the race overall had been drastically reduced. An estimated 300 had retired and 100 had been disqualified, mostly for taking lifts. Robinson held on to a lead of fifteen miles as he approached Fort William and Richard Penman had almost burnt himself out by the time Grundy overtook him. Robinson extended his lead to thirty miles over the next few days reaching Callander 280 miles from the start by 2nd March. Such was his pace that Butlin's mobile check points were having to leapfrog each other to keep pace with him. Grundy was tenaciously hanging on to second place but he was limping badly, having picked up a knock to his ankle which was stopping him from running. Ten miles behind him Bob Powell from Liverpool, a twenty-six year-old assistant chemist, had taken third place while Richard Penman had dropped out.

THE MARATHON WALKING CRAZE AND the Butlin Race in particular offered a great opportunity for advertising and commercial sponsorship. Heinz had a Mobile Soup Kitchen serving hot tomato soup to walkers and there was hot milk available from the Milk Marketing Board van. Welch's glucose sweets, Gale's honey, Soreen malt loaf and Adam's butter were also giving handouts to racers. In addition to making supplies available on the road, Adam's promised a year's supply of butter for the winner and a month's supply for anyone who finished within the subsequent forty-eight hours. Smith and Nephew, the makers of Elastoplast, had a mobile first aid van, Elliman's Foot Ointment and Muscle Rub was on hand to ease weary limbs and none of the male competitors had to look scruffy as Phillishave were loaning out battery razors. The Dunlop Rubber Company had fifty pairs of their 'Majesty Yachting Shoes' to give away and the Irwell Rubber Company had 100 plastic raincoats which they planned to hand out later in the race. These vans all followed the leading pack of walkers. Competitors further down the field, and no doubt more in need of these facilities, tended to miss out. By the time they arrived, the mobile canteens had packed up and moved on, following the leaders in order to be sure of press and the TV coverage.

Newspapers were also keen to get in on the act. The *News of the World* had previously sponsored 'The March of the Century' from Birmingham to London in December, but that hadn't been quite the publicity coup they'd hoped for. *The Empire News and Sunday Chronicle* had a mobile canteen and also claimed to have been recognised by the Butlin's Organisation as the 'Official Information Service' with their mobile information centre.

On Friday 26th February, just before the start of the race, the *Daily Sketch* announced it was funding a 'booster' prize for competitors. A £10 cash prize would be awarded with an embroidered satin sash (a perfect photo opportunity for news cameramen) to each man and woman who produced the best performance of the day.

The first winner of the *Daily Sketch* prize was the unstoppable David Robinson. On Monday 29th March, John Grundy won the sash and £10 prize for covering the ground between Fort Augustus and Fort William in five hours and twenty-three minutes, at an average speed just under six miles an hour. And Mrs Ashley won the women's prize for walking between Argay and Dingwall in twelve hours and twenty minutes.

FOR ALL THE GREAT AND the good's concern about the extreme weather in the north, road traffic was a far bigger hazard to the competitors. Wendy Lewis, joint favourite for the women's race, was hit a glancing blow from a car which sped off and didn't stop. She was spun around and knocked off her feet. Obviously upset and crying she needed to take a short rest before she felt fit to carry on walking.

Her arrival in Fort William was, by contrast, a much happier experience. She was leading the women's race at this point when she was met by Duncan Grant, the town Provost. He kissed her on the cheek, placed his chain of office around her neck and made her an honorary provost announcing, 'The town is yours for the day!' Honoured as Wendy no doubt felt, she wasn't lingering in Fort William to enjoy her new, if temporary civic status, and was soon back on the road and heading for Crianlarich, keen to maintain her lead over Beryl Randle.

The Provost of Fort William, entering into the spirit of the walk, was indicative of how the public at large viewed the Butlin Race. The press, with nowhere to sleep at John O'Groats and now struggling to keep pace with the leaders, hadn't warmed to the race and the authorities in the far north had been thoroughly frosty about it; but the British public, who love nothing more than a good competition and a plucky competitor or two, had taken it to their hearts. The public mood was summed up by Annie Skibuits from Mill Hill in North West London, who wrote to the *Daily Mail* letters page. She described the walkers as, 'The fun-makers.'

'Why, instead of applauding Mr Billy Butlin, do people carp and cavil? It's men like him – and the valiant marathon walkers – who put some colour and fun into what would otherwise become a drab and standardised world.'

No doubt the four men who proposed marriage to Wendy Lewis before she had even left the Highlands also thought they were entering into the fun of it all. Wendy, having turned down these prospective suitors, reached Crianlarich on Thursday 3rd March, day six of the race. With a twenty mile lead over Beryl Randle, by this point she was in need of a stop. She rested for fourteen hours leaving the town just minutes before Beryl arrived. The lead swapped twice between them during the day with Beryl in front when they reached Callender and Wendy behind hobbling along with a sore ankle.

If Wendy Lewis was unimpressed by the number of marriage proposals she was collecting, love certainly seemed to be in the air for some of the other walkers who had either come as a couple or, in some cases, had met on the walk itself where romance blossomed. Jean Pringle from the Isle of Wight, wearing a headscarf and a transparent plastic mac over her race number of 637, strolled along the road towards Helmsdale hand in hand with Michael Raines from Palmers Green in London, wearing number forty-nine. Helen Richardson from Glasgow and John Styles from Liverpool were so in love they didn't seem to mind being 200 miles behind the race leaders; so taken was thirty year old Mark White, a salesman from Oxford, with June Ramsay, a masseuse, he told the *Daily Sketch*, 'We might be looking for a register office soon.' Frank Dayman from Salford and his girlfriend Sheila Dillin from Crewe said they were encouraging each other to keep going, and Carol Dodds from Salisbury and Len Morley from Poplar in London would soon need either a church or a registry office: they got engaged at John O'Groats before the start of the race and put their celebrations on hold until they reached Land's End.

MRS DOROTHY SCOTT, A FORTY-six year old widow from Liverpool wearing race number 1245, had a presence in the race yet nobody, least of all the race organisers, could quite pin her down. She had aspirations of becoming Britain's answer to Dr Moore. She set out to walk from John O'Groats to Land's End on 20th January but then seemed to have dropped off everyone's radar somewhere around Glencoe. She subsequently entered the Butlin race and early reports had her leading the women's race some five miles ahead of Wendy Lewis. When questioned, at first the Butlin team denied all knowledge of her, then race marshal Sam Rockett announced that she had been disqualified but was carrying on with the race on her own. After that she no longer appeared in the Butlin lists of runners and walkers, but she had not yet finished with her own long distance adventures. She would yet play a significant, and ultimately decisive, role in the final act of the British craze for marathon walking.

MISS LAVENIA WHIPPY FROM FIJI, the lady with the parasol, was the last to cross the border. Many miles ahead of her David Robinson had been the first to cross from Scotland into England at four in the afternoon on 4th March with walking Alf Rozentals not far behind him in second place. He had cut Robinson's lead down from forty-five to twenty-five miles and John Grundy was still in touch but struggling with an ankle strain. Nobody was looking much further back in the men's race, the press focussed almost exclusively on the three-way tussle between Robinson, Grundy and Rozentals. James Musgrave, still unnoticed, quietly slipped over the border in fifth place just as he'd always planned to do.

Thirty-eight year old Jimmy Musgrave, wearing race number 701, at five foot four inches stood only an inch taller than John Grundy and was ranked by some newspapers as a 100 to 1 outsider. Musgrave had led an eventful life. A merchant seaman for eighteen years, his ship had been torpedoed during the Second World War and he was only rescued after spending twenty hours in the water. He had a second brush with death during the Korean War when he was a little too close for comfort to a boiler-room explosion. He then left the Merchant Marine and at the time of the race was working as a £10 per week glass packer for Pilkington Brothers Limited at Kirk Sandall near Doncaster. Even his friends admitted he didn't conform to the usual picture of an athlete. Short and stockily built, he would only admit to competing in a couple of merchant seamen's races in Africa. He enjoyed a pint of beer, the occasional cigarette and his friends said that he would never even walk as far as his local working men's club if he could get a lift. He'd dodged the media's attention so far and was being described as either a wildcard or a dark horse. He said later that John Grundy and Alf Rozentals had been too busy keeping an eye on each other to worry about him and they had failed to notice how he'd quietly progressed up the field. David Wathen (A. Walker) described Musgrave's race as 'scientific'. He had planned to cross the border into England in fifth place and then to gradually move up the field on the journey down through England and so be well placed to make a bid for the lead when he reached Cornwall.

THE *DAILY SKETCH* AWARDED ITS £10 daily prize for the best performance on 9th March to John Grundy and Wendy Lewis, and on the 10th March John Grundy and Beryl Randle took the prize. On 11th March Grundy won the prize for the third time in a row and Beryl for the second time.

By 28th February the Sunday newspaper *The People* estimated that 400 competitors had dropped out of the race and that there were somewhere in the region of 300 still competing. Along with their aches and pains those quitting had two main complaints. They felt that the trained and experienced road runners were taking over the race, leaving very little opportunity for the regular, 'have-a-go' kind of entrant and that these 'professional' runners with their sponsorship and support teams were at an unfair advantage. This was a valid point, although there was nothing in the rules to exclude support teams, trainers and pacemakers even if it didn't sit comfortably with the overall spirit of the race.

A bigger grouse was that competitors quickly became aware that not everyone was walking or running every inch of the way. Some contestants seemed to be under the impression that using your feet was optional. They were catching buses or taking lifts and more than twenty had already been disqualified. Here was a major headache for the organisers. It became clear that a substantial number of competitors were threatening the viability of the race as a whole by cheating on a grand scale.

Chapter Thirteen: Cheaters

THE GREAT BILLY BUTLIN WALK brought out the best in most people; grit, determination, courage, stick-ability, compassion and good humour. It served as a reminder of all of those qualities which are supposed to put the 'Great' in Great Britain. There was an element of the famous 'Dunkirk Spirit' about it, at a time when the Dunkirk beaches were still a recent memory. It was inevitable however that when large cash prizes were on offer, and the £1,000 first prize was a huge sum in 1960, there would always be those for whom the rewards of knowing you have done your best were not enough. Like the gambler who tries to knobble the favourite in a horse race, there will always be some who are tempted to cheat. And dishonesty in foot-races had a long and not very illustrious history.

Before Butlin's Walk, arguably the greatest foot-race in history was that of 'The Celebrated Captain Barclay' who, on Newmarket Heath, between June and July 1809, in what was hyped to be 'The Greatest Ever Sporting Event,' walked 1,000 miles in 1,000 hours for 1,000 guineas. Which sounds a pretty fair marathon in itself, especially when you consider 1,000 hours is just over forty-one and a half days. But no, Captain Barclay's challenge was much greater than that. He walked along a measured half mile track to a post where he would turn around and walk half a mile back; one mile every hour, night and day, for 1,000 hours.

This was the most sensational sporting event of its day and there were huge wagers laid as to the outcome. Rumour had it that with side-bets Barclay stood to make closer to 16,000 guineas (somewhere around six and a half million in today's money). However he was well aware that, with these amounts of cash in the offing, there was the very real danger that his record walk would be sabotaged by gamblers who had bet against him achieving this feat. So he could see to walk during the night and to avoid foul play, he arranged for gas lights to be mounted on poles along his route. Rival gamblers shot out these lights with musket balls. The danger became so intense that Barclay took to walking his measured mile with a brace of loaded pistols tucked in his belt and with ex-Champion prize-fighter Big John Gully by his side as a bodyguard. These measures paid off. He completed his walk, claimed his winnings and then took only the briefest of rests before he was fit to join his regiment and sail off to fight the wars against Napoleon.

On 6ᵀᴴ January 1960, just seven weeks before the Butlin Race, there had been a row over whether Terry Haywood from Birmingham had truly beaten Dr Moore's time from Edinburgh to London to win the £250 prize put up by garage owner Wilfred McDougall. Or, as van driver Bob Stenhouse claimed, Haywood had dishonestly taken a lift to Jedburgh. A Glaswegian typewriter mechanic called Kane later claimed to have unofficially beaten Dr Bab's time, as did Peter Hoy from Manchester, but after the Terry Haywood 'Jedgate' controversy the waters had become so muddied that nobody was awarded the prize.

From early on in the Billy Butlin Walk it became apparent to all involved that some competitors were cheating. Most did this by simply accepting a lift, or even hitching a lift in a car to speed them a few miles along the road and move them further up the ranks. One competitor was caught getting on a bus, and another particularly gullible fraudster was caught near Fort Augustus when he tried to hitch a lift in Billy Butlin's car. Honest walkers were outraged by these swindlers and complained, but the organisers had to catch them in the act before they could disqualify them, and catching the cheats was no easy task with competitors spread across most of Scotland and northern England. Also the speed of individual walkers could fluctuate wildly depending upon how tired they were and how long it was since they last stopped for a break.

As early as Sunday 28th February the *Empire News* was reporting that twenty racers had been disqualified for taking lifts. Ben Jones, in a letter home to his son David from Fort Augustus, was outraged by the dishonesty. 'There's more cheating going on here,' he wrote, 'than in any competition I've known.'

Some swindlers were more clever and more organised than others, arranging for their own car or van to pick them up, drive them along while they hid in the back, then to drop them a mile or so before the next checkpoint so they could walk up, have their card stamped and nobody would be any the wiser. If they had not been seen on the road by anyone they would simply say they had been resting in a house or a cottage along the way. It quickly became clear that the organisers needed to respond to this threat which could potentially make a mockery of the entire event.

Two of the more inventive frauds brought an old pram along, supposedly to hold their gear. Instead, when nobody was looking, one of them would ride in the pram while the other pushed: then later on they'd swap places.

Walkers push their gear along in an old pram.

Similar tactics were being used by the supposed 'ghost' walker. The *Daily Sketch* had picked up a rumour doing the rounds of one walker having a double. Some said they were identical twins racing as just one person. When one twin was tired, he would ride in a car while his twin put on his coat and race number and walked on in his place.

The race marshal, ex-cross Channel swimmer Sam Rockett, ordered his stewards and officials to be extra vigilant for evidence of cheating and he instituted a system of flying checkpoints in addition to the thirty-two static check points. Mobile checks would be set up between the regular ones with the hope of catching out cheats and marshals would become suspicious if they noted that a walker had suddenly covered an inordinate distance from their previously recorded position. A number of dishonest competitors were caught and disqualified this way.

Vehicles were also examined. Billy Butlin himself stopped and searched the support car from one of the national newspapers which had entered a reporter in the race. At first glance everything seemed above board until he opened the boot where he found the reporter curled up inside asleep.

Race officials established a temporary check point just beyond a section of the route which had become flooded after heavy rain. Any competitor who arrived with dry feet had clearly not walked through the flood and were summarily disqualified.

The issue of fraud became a major threat in the early stages of the walk and the more wily cheats became adept at spotting flying checkpoints, driving back down the road and dropping off the competitor who could then walk up as if nothing was amiss. Butlin responded by bringing in ever more mobile check points, even putting out a call to his fairground and amusement park friends to come and staff these additional check points.

The race officials clearly implemented a multi-pronged approach in an attempt to catch and disqualify unsporting swindlers. There was entrapment. Early in the race David Wathen writes about how a car would stop and offer the walker a lift; if this was refused the driver would ask for their race number. There may also have been spies amongst the participants. A rumour circulated that Billy Butlin had brought in fifty Redcoats disguised as race walkers. This move, if indeed it was ever more than just a colourful rumour, proved unsuccessful as the Redcoats, unused to race walking, only succeeded in catching each other. The most successful way of weeding out the cheats was undoubtedly the flying checkpoints, along with vigilance and common sense. If a walker missed a checkpoint, or had quickly covered an unexpectedly long distance, or arrived at a stop in foul conditions without looking as if they had been out in the weather, the official would smell a rat.

Wathen's anger at cheats was understandable. He, along with other honest competitors, was exhausting himself, coping with the privations of life on the road, putting in the long hours and even longer miles to try and reach Land's End, even when it was clear that they would not be amongst prize winners and were just walking because the race in itself had become important to them. He reserves a special contempt for those who took lifts in the early part of the race, avoiding what were probably the toughest conditions, establishing a good lead for themselves and then maintaining it. 'It is known,' he states, 'that some of these [cheats] became cautious and took advantage of their lead to stay in the race without further cheating. Just how many of them were still in the race when they reached Land's End will never be known.'

While anyone committing fraud angered the rank and file competitors it is doubtful that it had any meaningful effect on the overall results. The winners and those who took the major places were athletes of some standing, who were used to taking part in major sporting events and were familiar with having their performances come under scrutiny. Also the progress of the leaders was followed so closely by the press and race officials that cheating for them was never an option. Indeed Jimmy Musgrave, in third place on 11th March, commented on race scrutiny for the leaders. 'The security men,' he said, 'are breathing down our necks all the time.'

It seems unlikely, and indeed it would have been self-defeating, for those who were walking just for the challenge and experience of taking part in such a unique race would have had much of an urge to try and beat the system. For them the satisfaction of completing the course was the reward in itself and this would be of no value if they had taken a ride for any part of the distance. That only leaves those competing for the minor prizes. As Wathen says it is impossible to tell how many cheated early, avoided some of the toughest sections of the course, unfairly grabbed a good head start then stopped cheating when the organisers clamped down and so made a good time to the finish. Yet this seems doubtful. If the mindset is to cheat it is unlikely that a third of the way into the race they would have a change of heart and become a model law-abiding race walker, especially if only competing for a minor prize.

MOST OF THE BUTLIN RACE walkers were honest and would never have dreamt of playing unfairly. Their day to day existence of a life on the road was that of an itinerant: a rover, a wanderer, a tramp; living rough, bivouacking, sleeping under hedges and enjoying such meals as they could get whenever they could get them. And always, always putting in the miles. It was a life of sore feet, blisters, aching muscles and bone weary tiredness alternated with the occasional good times when everything was going well, when they felt strong, fit, and the miles simply slipped by. It was a time of easy friendships which would quickly form and just as quickly be dissolved when one friend dropped out or another put on a burst of speed and their paths would never cross again.

For all the talk of scroungers who dropped out with no means of paying their way home or those who expected the organisers to feed them, most walkers had come prepared with snacks, chocolate and hot drinks to keep them going and cash to pay their way. Even the strongest walker could not carry all of their provisions for the entire race in a rucksack, so most bought meals as and where they could in cafes, hotels and pubs along the way. The average Butlin race walker paid somewhere in the region of £30 for their race expenses overall.

Where to sleep was a constant problem. Village halls, schools and seamen's missions were opened up along the route to provide shelter and there the walkers would just doss down wherever they could find a few inches of floor space. Farmers were usually happy to let walkers sleep in their barns, and very often they would cook them a substantial breakfast next morning to give them a good start. Numerous good-hearted people took competitors in, and sometimes the walkers themselves would find inventive places to lay their head. David Wathen once had a good night's sleep on the back seat of what he assumed to be an abandoned car. He was woken in the early hours in something of a panic when the car started to rock alarmingly on its suspension. His first thought was that the car's owner had come back and he was going to drive away with him still recumbent on the backseat. Instead it turned out to be another competitor who had also found the abandoned motor and was climbing in for a kip. Wathen decided it was time he got back on the road anyway so gave up the backseat to the newcomer and set off walking again. Another enterprising walker was passing a half-built house one night and found a roll of linoleum inside waiting to be fitted. He positioned one end of the roll against the house wall to stop the wind blowing through then crawled inside and had a wonderful night's sleep.

Chapter Fourteen: Four Walkers

YOUNG JOHN ALEXANDER (ALEX) Dick was never quite sure what made him apply for the Billy Butlin Walk. It certainly wasn't any sort of background in sports or athletics. Somehow the romance, the excitement and the unique experience of the walk appealed to him. Plus at that time it seemed like everyone and his dog were setting out to make marathon walks. He was seventeen in 1960 and still in the early stages of an engineering apprenticeship in Glasgow.

There were a number of hurdles to be overcome before he could even think about entering the walk. Firstly his mates and the other apprentices ribbed him mercilessly for even thinking about going. 'Yea'll never make it,' they told him. 'They'll bring you back in bits and pieces and we'll no be able to put yea back together again.' But this only made him all the more determined. He'd show them. Then he had to get permission from work to release him from his apprenticeship for two or three weeks to take part. They proved quite understanding and quickly granted him their blessing. Lastly, he had a much tougher obstacle to overcome. He had to persuade his mother.

Like most mothers, Mrs Dick was only concerned about young Alex's welfare. Able and confident he may have been but he was no runner and he'd never shown much of an aptitude or an interest in taking part in sports or athletics. She was worried as to how he'd cope with the 895 miles to Land's End. Alex wheedled and pleaded until finally his mother set him a challenge. If he could walk from their home in Inchinnan, on the outskirts of Glasgow, to Greenock and back again, a distance of

John Alex Dick

about thirty miles, she would let him go. Young Alex jumped at the chance.

Next day he set off striding out alongside the Forth of Clyde on a wild and breezy day. Four hours brisk walking saw him in Greenock, by which time he felt Butlin Race or not he'd had enough walking for one day. The bus back to Glasgow pulled in. It seemed silly to just let it go so he hopped on and rode all the way back to Inchinnan. When he got there he hung around for an hour or more at the top of the farm lane to kill a bit of time then he went home and told his Mum that he'd walked there and back. So she let him go on the Butlin Walk.

When the rockets were set off for the start of the race, young Alex's competitive instincts kicked in and he pressed on ahead, made a good start and was near the front of the pack that first night when after a mild start the weather turned foul. The wind got up, the rain lashed down and the hail stones were so bad they cut his skin, leaving his face bleeding. By the time he'd reached Lybster, about seventeen miles from the start, he decided it was time to take a break. He managed to find lodgings in the village where a lady gave him a meal and a bed for the remainder of the night. When he woke up the next morning he was so stiff he thought rigor mortis had set in. He could hardly move let alone walk.

He thought that his race was over after just one day. What on earth would his apprentice mates say, and more to the point what would his mother say? But he hadn't allowed for the resourcefulness of the people in the far north of Scotland. The lady of the house knew exactly what to do. She ran a steaming hot bath and dunked him in it; let the hot peaty water work its magic on his stiff aching muscles; dried him off, helped him get dressed and sent him on his way. Another one of Billy Butlin's End to Enders was back into the fray.

If anything, day two was even tougher for Alex. The hot bath had got his body moving again but there was to be no jogging or even trying to keep up with the leaders. On that second day he was moving so slowly it took him two hours to cover the first mile.

Most walkers tried to keep the amount of kit they carried to a minimum and Alex was no exception. He wore a leather jacket, a pair of Dunlop boots and kept on the same set of clothes throughout the trek. He even dumped the small rucksack he had set off with early on, because he felt it was weighing him down. David Wathen (A. Walker) commented on how many rucksacks, clothes, vacuum flasks and all sorts of kit had been jettisoned, just left along the roadside during the first few days of the walk. He added local people must have done rather well out of this unexpected windfall.

When the weather turned bad, as it often did, Alex, along with all the other walkers, simply got wet. They were regularly soaked through and the wind would dry their clothes on them. Keeping going kept them tolerably warm and occasionally when they stayed at houses along the route, the lady of the house would wash and dry their kit overnight. This became a necessity one night for Alex. A farmer let him sleep in his barn and, exhausted after a long day on the road, young Alex bedded down in some soft sweet straw and was quickly sound asleep. Next morning was something of a horrific awakening. The cattle in the barn were not penned up but free to roam and roam they did freely spreading fresh cow dung all over the barn, the straw and Alex. The farmer's wife, possibly a bit embarrassed about their cows' behaviour, let him have a bath, washed his gear and fed him breakfast before she sent him on his way.

Most of the time he was able to find someone to take him in and let him have a bed for the night. He only had to pay for his lodgings once and that was at Shap in Cumbria (Cumberland as it was then). Spectators and supporters along the way would often buy them a meal or give them some sweets or a bit of spare cash. One young lady Alex met gave him a St Christopher on a chain to wear around his neck to keep him safe on his journey.

As he progressed down the country the stiffness of the second day wore off and he gradually became fitter and more able to cope with the big distances he was walking. By the time he had reached the Midlands he was covering an average of forty plus miles each day and on one momentous occasion between Taunton and Bodmin he walked and jogged more than seventy miles in a single day. He estimated that he walked for ninety-five percent of the distance and ran for the other five percent.

If the Ord of Caithness was the crunch section for the early part of the walk, Bodmin Moor was the sting in the tail for when the walkers reached Cornwall. All walkers found this high exposed stretch of moorland challenging. It would even be the deciding factor in both the men's and the women's race. Alex trekked over Bodmin Moor at night which he found a pretty scary and eerie experience. By this time he had made friends with twenty-three year old Alan Cox from London. They reached Land's End together at ten past eight on the morning of Monday 21st March, completing the race in twenty-three days, fifteen hours and ten minute,s coming sixty-first and sixty-second in the race standings overall.

If Alex Dick couldn't take the £1,000 prize for the men's race, he had hoped to win the £100 prize as the youngest competitor. Even here he was to be disappointed. That prize went to Robert Seales from Swindon, even though he came in thirty-two places behind Alex and more than three days later.

Although he missed out on a prize, Alex had at least won out in terms of bragging rights. He had proved his mates wrong, had justified his mother's faith in him and was treated as a returning hero when he got back home to Inchinnan. He was even featured in the local paper and on the Pathe News.

THE BUTLIN WALK EXPERIENCE OF Michael Green was similar in a number of ways to that of Alex Dick. He had also hoped to win the prize for the youngest competitor but again missed out to Robert Seales, and like Alex, was also an apprentice engineer.

He caught the train from his home in Aylesbury, Buckinghamshire to Wick and then rode on one of the double decker buses specially laid on for the event to John O'Groats. He remembers standing there with hundreds of other competitors waiting for the start and watching Billy Butlin fly in by helicopter.

The first night was vile weather, and as his kit consisted of a tracksuit and a groundsheet he also got soaked. Like Alex, it was a dogged determination to finish, 'pig-headedness' Michael called it, which kept him going. He couldn't face the idea of returning home and not having reached the end. What would his engineering apprentice mates or his family have said? He would never have lived it down.

The spectators and the supporters along the way were very kind, he said. They turned out in their thousands to cheer them along and would help in any way they could. Often they would put him up for the night or buy him a cup of tea along the way. Once he remembers a lorry driver stopping his truck to give him a sandwich. When he wore out the soles of his boots someone in the crowd took him along to a nearby shoe shop where the cobbler quickly glued on a new set of soles and heels, no charge.

Michael Green. After reaching Land's End he walked home to Aylesbury.

Some nights he spent in barns or he would wrap himself up in his groundsheet and sleep under a hedge. At one point, hoping to lighten his load, Michael arranged for his rucksack to be sent on ahead, but

125

somehow it went astray and didn't catch-up with him until weeks later, when the walk was over.

The course route wasn't always very clear and sometimes you had to use your own initiative. It was always galling to take a wrong turn and find you had to backtrack five or six miles to get back onto the approved route. This was important; Michael didn't want to miss a checkpoint. Butlin's officials were very keen to keep track of competitors, once cheating and taking lifts became a problem. Then there were the roving checkpoints which would just pop up in unexpected places and stamp your race card.

Michael arrived at Land's End at four pm on Wednesday 23rd of March 1960. He was still more than a day ahead of the youngest competitor, he had not won any prize money, but he felt a great sense of achievement. Sadly a sense of achievement wouldn't buy him a train ticket home and by this stage he had no money left. There was nothing else for it. He had walked there, and he'd have to walk back; which is just what he did, almost 300 miles back home to Aylesbury.

FORTY-FOUR YEAR OLD JACK Roston Williams from Shrewsbury had more in common with Dr Barbara Moore than with young apprentices Alex Dick and Michael Green. He had been born a farmer's son but had experienced considerable health problems as a child which stopped him being able to run and play with other children. His eyesight was poor and he had pains in his bones, joints and especially his feet. When he was a young man his doctor advised him to travel to a warm climate, such as Egypt, where the sun and heat would hopefully relieve his symptoms. While on a boat sailing to the Mediterranean, he became friends with a couple who told him about the benefits of health foods. He began to follow their advice, eating a healthy and primarily a vegetarian diet, and discovered not only a form of relief for his problems but also a new career.

On his return to England he continued to eat a healthy diet and opened a health foods shop. The shop was a success and as his business expanded he was able to add treatment rooms, and later, a hotel specialising in healthy eating. So prominent was he on the health foods scene that Dr Barbara Moore herself once stayed at his hotel when she was addressing a meeting. It was just shortly after his wife Ruth had given birth to their daughter, and Dr Barbara told her that her special diet had kept her own body so fit that she would be able to have a baby, if she chose to, when she was 100 years old.

A friend encouraged Jack to go in for the Butlin Walk. They were going to enter together but at the last minute his friend backed out and went to Australia instead. Jack was a regular walker but not a racer or an athlete. He was keen to take part just to see how well he could do, especially in view of the health problems he'd had since childhood. He wanted to prove to himself that he could walk from John O'Groats to Land's End.

Prior to setting off he bought himself a new pair of shoes for the walk. He had extra wide feet and the only shoes he found comfortable were from a shop in Baker Street. Despite not having the chance to break these new shoes in they performed magnificently. He suffered no blisters and they had worn so little that even by the end of the race it was still possible to read the makers name on the sole of the shoe.

With his special vegetarian and healthy diet, finding the right food on the walk was more of a problem for Jack than it was for most walkers. It wasn't easy locating fresh fruit and vegetables in the far north of Scotland in February, and whilst he could carry some food with him in his rucksack, he had to keep the weight he carried down to a minimum. One option was to forage along the hedgerows for nettles and fresh shoots, and sometimes farmers would let him dig up a few carrots from their fields.

He was also less fortunate than Alex or Michael when it came to finding accommodation along the way. Jack opted for a slow and steady approach to the Butlin Walk so he was never up with the leaders. By the time he reached town a considerable amount of walkers and runners had already passed through, and as many of these had stayed in people's homes and left without offering to pay, thus when Jack arrived they were reluctant to take him in. He camped out quite a lot and stayed with a friend near Gretna when he reached the Scottish border. Ruth was able to meet up with him on a couple of occasions, and they stayed in a bed and breakfast just north of Preston, then later in Shropshire and finally, just before he reached the finish at Land's End.

Alex Dick was not the only walker to suffer from stiffness on the walk. There were times, especially setting off in the mornings, when Jack

Williams's legs were so stiff the only way he could make any progress at all was to use both hands to grab hold of his trouser leg just above the knee then physically haul his legs forward one at a time.

Despite his muscle problems, dietary restrictions and lack of accommodation he remained determined throughout and arrived at Land's End at six-thirty-five pm on Wednesday 23rd March, just an hour and thirty-five minutes behind Michael Green and in a very creditable ninety-first place out of the 715 starters.

THERE WAS NEVER ANY DOUBT that twenty-eight year old Duncan Gillies from Keith in Banffshire would compete in the Great Billy Butlin Race. Not only that, he hoped to win. Duncan had built up a reputation locally as a walker and runner and had recently beaten fifty-two other competitors to win the nine mile marathon walk from Rhynie to Castle Park, Huntly, in a time of one hour and forty-two minutes.

Yet taking part in the Butlin Walk would require considerable sacrifices. He worked as a farmhand, lived in a tied cottage and had a growing family. He was given four weeks leave from his job to take part but it also meant four weeks with no wages.

Like most of the other racers he took minimal kit and had no support team. He wore baseball boots as he did for most of his races, and had a jacket which was as waterproof as any coat was in those days before Gore-Tex fabrics. He carried a small knapsack and a sleeping bag.

One evening he was walking along a remote stretch of road by the shores of Loch Ness when night fell. There were no houses around where he could ask for lodgings and as it was a fine night he decided to bivouac. He found a cosy spot amongst the heather on the steep bank between the road and the loch, climbed into his sleeping bag and was soon asleep. He woke next morning to the sound of water lapping and found he was only a few feet from the water's edge. Cocooned in his sleeping bag and fast asleep he'd rolled down the bank in the night.

He was part of the leading pack from the start but began to slip down the field when he had to stop to find his meals and somewhere to stay.

Duncan Gillies

This was where competitors like John Grundy and Alf Rozentals who had pacemakers and back-up teams had the advantage because they didn't have to use valuable time and energy to organise meals and accommodation. Duncan was hugely impressed by David Robinson, the research student from the London School of Economics, who was the only one amongst the early leaders with no support team. 'David Robinson just kept on going,' said Duncan. 'He never stopped.'

Indeed it may have been trying to emulate Robinson that was Duncan's undoing. He also tried to just keep on going. He pressed on even when his baseball boots were wearing smooth. He kept going when the soles wore right through and even then he didn't stop as he started to wear off the skin the undersides of his feet. Finally he had to stop and needed to spend a day in hospital just to give his feet the chance to heal. Losing a day in hospital put his race so far back that he lost any chance of being amongst the prizes, but he kept going anyway.

Duncan arrived at Land's End on Saturday 19th March at 10.20pm, in fiftieth place. If he hadn't lost a day while he was in hospital he would have been in fortieth place and still out of the prizes. It was a bitter pill to swallow, for a poorly paid farmworker to give up a month's wages, put in a huge effort, and still miss out on any prize money, but worse was to follow. He found himself in a similar position to young Michael Green. He'd used up all his cash by the time he reached Land's End so, like Michael, he set off to walk home, all the way back to Scotland if necessary.

Instead he just walked as far as London, a little over 300 miles, where one of his brothers lived. The brother was an inspector for the railways. Duncan stayed with him for a few days and he bought Duncan a railway ticket home.

Once Duncan arrived back home his family could see how gaunt he had become. It was even possible to count his ribs. Despite his thinness and losing a month's wages, Duncan never regretted competing in the Billy Butlin Race. Just like the families of Alex Dick, Michael Green and Jack Williams, Duncan's relatives were proud of what he had achieved. It was a one-off event, the chance of a lifetime and they were part of the 138 competitors who completed the race within the twenty-eight day time limit. Duncan had his certificate framed and it hung on the wall of his cottage for years.

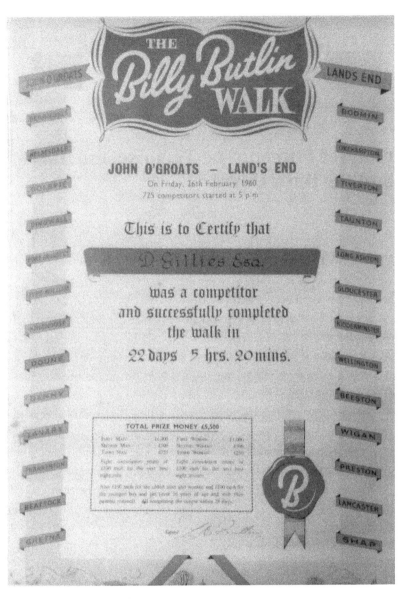

Duncan Gillies's race certificate.

Chapter Fifteen: The Tortoise, the Hare and the Dark Horse

BY 7TH MARCH WALKERS WERE spread out across the country from the Highlands of Scotland to the West Country. Billy Butlin and his race stewards were at full stretch to try to marshal them all, so he sent a message to the tail enders that as they stood no chance of being amongst the prizes it was time for them to give up and go home. The marchers responded in short order telling him they were enjoying the race, they didn't care about the money, and they were continuing on.

Despite Wendy Lewis having the highest profile in the Women's Race, by 10th March it was Beryl Randle who held a slight lead as indeed she had for most of the race. She gained a little more ground later in the day when Wendy stopped first for a medical check-up and then, as it was her nineteenth birthday, for a longer than usual lunch break and a celebration meal of roast chicken washed down by a glass of champagne.

There were still several racers in the running for the men's event. Alf Rozentals was leading but was overtaken by John Grundy at Gloucester during the night. Musgrave was in third place, but for David Robinson his burst of speed early in the race had taken its toll and he had dropped down the field. Bookmakers in Grundy's home town of Wakefield were so confident that he would win they had stopped taking bets on him.

Soon after, just north of Pawlett in Somerset, Alf Rozentals's brother was knocked off his bicycle by a lorry and sustained injuries sufficiently serious for him to need to go to hospital. Once again it was road traffic which posed the greatest danger for walkers, their supporters, and race organisers. Rozentals stayed with his brother while the ambulance came with no thought for the race time he was losing. After this incident he seemed to lose some of his enthusiasm for the walk.

By this late stage in the race, even the winners of the *Daily Sketch* £10 for the best performance of the day was becoming somewhat predictable and confined to the leaders in both the men's and the women's races. On Saturday 12th March it was won by Jim Musgrave and Wendy Lewis; the following day John Grundy and Beryl Randle took the prize. But there were no cheery photos anymore of the winners posing with their sash: the racers were either too busy sleeping or they were pressing on down the road.

An exception to this was on 7th March, day ten of the race. Ben Jones, the Electricity Generating Board linesman from South Wales, walking the whole way in his Wellington boots, won the £10 prize for the day's best performance in the men's race, covering eighty-two miles in twenty-four hours. He had become something of a hit with the press by this time. Like David Robinson, he was doing the walk unsupported and the press had taken to calling him 'The Duke of Wellingtons' or 'Ben the Boots'. For most competitors, participating in the race was a blow to their finances. Ben had set off from John O'Groats with £20 in his pocket, but this had eroded down to just thirty-five shillings. Winning the £10 daily prize meant he didn't have to worry about affording food, or a bed.

Ben Jones's sash from The Daily Sketch for the best performance on day ten.

On Friday 11th March the *Daily Mail* likened the contest between Grundy and Rozentals to that of the tortoise and the hare with the headline, 'It's Odds On Billy Butlin's Hare.' John Grundy, who had run most of the way, was the hare and Alf Rozentals, who steadfastly refused to run and would only walk was the tortoise. By the following day Jim Musgrave had upset these predictions: the race was now between the tortoise, the hare, and Musgrave as the 'dark horse'. Alternately running and walking, Musgrave had reached Oakhampton in Devon at 12:21 in the morning. 'I think I can spare myself a bit of respite in Oakhampton,' he said. 'That does not mean I am going to go to sleep though, [it means] a good meal. Then I hope to press on more or less non-stop.'

For all Musgrave's confidence, the sternest test lay ahead. As the racers crossed into Cornwall, Grundy and his team didn't believe that Musgrave would be able to keep his blistering pace going all the way to Land's End. The previous day he had overtaken both Grundy and Rozentals and then stretched out a lead, but it was not humanly possible he could carry on to Land's End without another rest stop When that happened it would be Grundy's opportunity to move into the lead.

In this respect John Grundy, with all of his marathon experience was correct, as was Jim Musgrave, who had run his 'scientific race'. But their reasoning failed to take into account two vital factors. On the one hand it was the first time a race like this had ever been run and there was nothing to compare it with. A twenty-six mile marathon pales into insignificance against the 891 mile Butlin Race. Neither runner truly knew quite how far he had pushed himself or how much he had left in the tank. The second factor was that Bodmin Moor, lashed by wind and rain, still lay ahead.

Out on Bodmin Moor, on that stormy March night, John Grundy and James Musgrave would discover the limits of their strength and endurance. Marathon runners have a term for when their strength and energy gives out: they call it 'hitting the wall.' That night Grundy and Musgrave didn't so much hit the wall, they slammed into it.

Musgrave had not slept for twenty-four hours and had made a superhuman effort to reach the front. Grundy was still going, despite being injured and needing heavy strapping on his right leg. They both reached the point in those vile weather conditions where neither of them could go on any further and they both collapsed at the side of the road.

Their supporters helped them up, offered words of encouragement and massaged their stiff and aching muscles. Chris Brasher, reporting on the race for the *Guardian*, later likened the courage and tenacity of Musgrave and Grundy with the best of the athletic performances at the Rome Olympics.

John Grundy (127) who came second and a group of school children near Tavistock.

With the two leaders out of action, the outcome of the race hung in the balance. Who would recover first? And once they had recovered, who would still muster the strength to race the last fifty miles to Land's End? There, Billy Butlin, the world's press, and a cheque for £1,000 were waiting.

It is evident from their performances that Grundy and his team, along with Musgrave and his team, understood about fitness, training, and the physical preparation needed for a contest of this type. Yet winning depends as much on psychological preparation and self-belief as physical fitness. With both competitors exhausted and unable to run any further the psychological recovery could be the pivotal factor and it was here that Jim Musgrave had the luck.

Grundy had been right in one respect: exhaustion did strike Musgrave down some fifty miles out from the finish, but it also struck Grundy at the same time. Unknowingly both runners collapsed just a few hundred yards from each other in the dark of Bodmin Moor. As Grundy was helped from the pub where he had taken shelter to a nearby house where he would have a bath, a meal and a short rest, he was spotted by one of Musgrave's support team. When the news that Grundy was no more than a couple of hundred yards away and temporarily out of action was passed on to Jim Musgrave it had an effect on the runner something like the application of an electric cattle prod. Musgrave, who a few moments before was unable to go a step further and was telling his supporters he was going to drop out, was on his feet in an instant and jogging away into the night his heart set on being the first man to reach Land's End.

John Grundy took a much needed two hour break for his bath and a meal so that by the time he was back on the road Musgrave had stretched out a five mile lead. But the race was not over. In a stunning burst of speed Grundy pursued Musgrave whittling away at his lead and he came close to overhauling him until, in the depths of the night, his legs gave way for the second time and he keeled over onto the grass at the side of the road. 'Take me home,' he said, 'I've failed you, I'm sorry.' Musgrave may have had the legs on John Grundy but he had failed no one. His supporters got him back on his feet and, limping heavily, he walked the last twenty-six miles to Land's End with his pacemaker.

THE CROWDS HAD BEEN GATHERING before dawn at Land's End, keen to be there to witness the climax of the Great Billy Butlin Race. The media were out in force. An impromptu stage had been built from two farm carts, with beer crates for steps and drapes to hide its rustic construction. Battalions of police had been brought in from all across the West Country to control the spectators who had swelled into the thousands and were now thronging the last mile of the route.

Even at this late stage it was far from certain who would win. Rumour and speculation was rife. Would it be marathon runner John Grundy, the long-time race favourite, or Musgrave the wildcard from Doncaster?

In the pale dawn light on Sunday 13th March 1960 the crowds were rewarded by the sight of the small but sturdy figure of Jimmy Musgrave, flat cap on his head, as he trotted purposely towards the winning post and then, without even breaking step, straight up the steps of the makeshift dais to shake hands with Billy Butlin and receive his check for £1,000. He had covered the 891 miles from John O'Groats, through the toughest winter conditions, in fifteen days, fourteen hours and thirty-one minutes, walking and jogging the last 103 miles in fourteen hours and thirty-one minutes with only a fifteen minute break on Bodmin Moor when he had been struck down with the cramps.

Race winner Jim Musgrave (701) wearing cap.

Amidst the popping of flashbulbs Musgrave was photographed by the iconic Land's End signpost, being presented with his £1,000 cheque by Billy Butlin. He declined a civic lunch asking instead for a hot bath, which he promptly fell asleep in, but he roused himself to be up and dressed again in order to be there to cheer John Grundy home one hour and twenty-three minutes later.

Alfred Rozentals, the Nottinghamshire miner who had walked the entire way, came in third four hours and twenty-five minutes later. The crowd was thinning by this time, but his wife Jean and seven year old daughter Susan were waiting for him at Land's End. As soon as she saw him, young Sue ran out from the crowd and sprang into her dad's arms and he carried her with him as he crossed the finishing line.

Alfred Rozentals, the man who refused to run and would only walk. He came third.

The fourth man home did not arrive until 10:52 the following morning. This was forty-five year old Victor Burr from Coventry wearing race number 1195. He was followed half an hour later by forty-six year old Benjamin Jones wearing number 559 from Swansea, the man who had walked the whole way in a pair of Wellington boots. His years of walking big distances every day following the powerlines in South Wales had proved to be the perfect training. He was the highest finisher with no support team, or 'a lone ranger' as Billy Butlin called him. Butlin was so impressed with Ben's walk that he laid-off a £100 bet against himself that Ben couldn't walk the whole way in wellies. His winnings went to Ben as a bonus so Ben won £200 in total. Butlin went to meet him and they walked the last four miles together. An RAF doctor examined Ben's feet after his walk. He may have worn the heels of his Wellington boots completely down but he had no blisters and his feet were in perfect condition.

Ben Jones with his famous Wellies awarded the Dunlop Prize.

Of the early finishers, only John Grundy attended the civic lunch. He told reporters he planned to use his £500 prize for second place to fund a trip to New Zealand. Jim Musgrave and his two man support team were keen to get away and back to Doncaster as soon as the festivities had started to die down. 'I'm clocking on at work six o'clock tomorrow morning,' he told reporters with something of a gleam in his eye. 'And I don't want to be late.'

THE TINY SOUTH YORKSHIRE PIT village of Dunscroft had never known anything quite like it. The streets were decked with flags and bunting and almost all of the 5,000 residents turned out to welcome Jim and his support team home.

Three men from the village had decided to enter the race just a fortnight before the start. They were Richard Dixon, twenty-nine, John Andrew Ather, twenty-seven, plus Jim Musgrave; and Patrick Carlin, their trainer. They took two weeks holiday from their job at Pilkington's Glass Works and initially agreed to share any winnings. Later they revised this plan and agreed that anyone who won prize money should keep what was left after covering the expenses. Injury forced Richard

Dixon and John Ather to drop out quite early in the race but they agreed to stay on and act as pacemakers for Musgrave.

Jim and his co-workers were in for a surprise when they returned to work: their boss, Sir Harry Pilkington, was a sports fan who had warmed to their achievement. He granted them a fortnight's holiday to make up for the leave they had to take to compete in the race.

The celebration started grandly with the Hatfield Main Colliery band leading a procession along Dunscroft main street and children being allowed out of school early to cheer and wave flags. Matters quickly got out of hand, and the celebration turned into something more like a minor riot. Jim, a bachelor, lodged with his cousin Mrs Mary Miller, and at one point there were fifty or more people all trying to push their way into the house. Windows were broken and the fences of houses on either side were trampled flat. When the stair carpet was ripped up and the television set almost came to grief the formidable Mrs Miller ordered everyone out of the house.

Such was the press of people in the house that Jim, despite being the hero of the hour, wasn't able to get out to attend his own welcome home party. He had to resort to climbing out of a back upstairs window and shinning down the drainpipe into the garden before he could escape over the fence. He then met all of his friends at the Dunscroft Working Men's Social Club where the party really started.

Chapter Sixteen: Celebrations and a Plunge from the Rooftop

WHILE RIOTOUS TIMES WERE BEING had in Doncaster, back in Cornwall the Women's Race was finally reaching its climax. In a strange symmetry, just like the Men's Race, it was again a case of the outsider, the young pretender, snatching victory from the race favourite. And once again Cornwall's Bodmin Moor was to play a pivotal part.

It's questionable whether competitors could be said to be neck and neck when they are in fact both asleep in separate rooms of the same hotel, yet this was the position in the early hours of Monday 14th March. Beryl Randle and Wendy Lewis were sixty-five miles from Land's End, and both were resting in Cornwall's famous Jamaica Inn. Beryl was the first to leave, taking to the road at three am. Wendy, suffering from a build-up of fluid in her legs, slept on for another hour and twenty-five minutes. Beryl stepped out holding onto the lead until just thirty miles before the finish but by eight in the morning when she reached Cambourne her old ankle trouble flared up and she was forced to stop and rest it. Wendy passed her at nine-forty-five but was in such a dazed state that she didn't know she had taken a four mile lead until someone amongst a group of spectators told her.

The crowds at Land's End exceeded even those who only forty-two days earlier had cheered home Dr Barbara Moore. Just after midnight on Tuesday 15th March a team of Billy Butlin's men formed a guard of honour around Wendy Lewis and marched the last mile with her to prevent her from being mobbed by the crowd. Billy Butlin himself led a chorus of the 'Happy Wanderer' as she arrived at the winning post at twelve-thirty. Her time was seventeen days and seven hours, slashing six days off her previous John O'Groats to Land's End time that she had set just thirty-eight days before. She was helped up onto the impromptu stage and presented with her cheque for £1,000 by Billy Butlin.

'I feel wonderful,' said Wendy. 'First I want a great big meal. I don't care what it is. I've had nothing but nuts and raisins all day. Then I would like a bath. And then bed.'

WITH THE SPOTLIGHT ON WENDY Lewis, Beryl Randle's arrival at Land's End some eight hours later was a muted affair by contrast. The crowds had departed and there were few press or TV cameras still around. But Billy Butlin, who had immense admiration for the grit and courage shown by both women, wanted to ensure that Beryl received the recognition she deserved. When it was clear she wasn't going to win, and in view of the pain she had been experiencing with her ankle he sent her a message asking her to rest and delay her arrival so that he could be there in person to welcome her. A mile from home she took a short break to have a wash, put on some make-up and change into a clean blouse and her international blazer, so that she finished looking as good as it was possible for someone who had just walked and run the length of the country in seventeen days and sixteen hours. Yet it must have been a bitter pill for her to swallow. All through the walk she had been confronted with crowds chanting 'We want Wendy!' And at Land's End after the crowds had departed she had to walk under banners emblazoned, 'Welcome Wendy'.

If Dr Barbara Moore had been dubbed the 'Soviet Woman's Heroine' in Russia, then brave Beryl Randle deserved to be called 'Britain's Woman's Heroine'. Except in England we don't do things like that, and especially not in the 1960s. Instead Billy Butlin showed his admiration for her in a more direct and tangible way. He doubled her prize money from £500 to £1,000.

WHEN THE CHEERS DIED DOWN, and after they had been presented with their cheques, the Billy Butlin racers wanted just three things: a meal, a bath and a good long sleep. After the press had their fill of shots of haggard and exhausted looking walkers, celebrations were put on hold until the next morning.

After breakfast there were yet more newspaper interviews and photos; Wendy and Beryl being given a tour of Land's End each being carried by a big burly man, Wendy and Beryl walking along, somewhat gingerly wearing soft carpet slippers on their feet. Even after a good sleep the exhaustion still showed on both of their faces. And finally Wendy and Beryl embracing. A good degree of camaraderie had built up between the two women on the walk.

Beryl's husband Ronald, an oil representative, and her boss Mr A. Grayson, managing director of a brake lining company in the Midlands, had been there at the end to cheer her home and the next day they set off on the journey back to Walsall. Nineteen year old Wendy, who the press had made into the star of the walk, was still the centre of media attention. What was she going to spend her winnings on? she was asked. 'I'm going to open a hairdressing salon with my sisters Joy and Angel,' she said. And what did you think about during all the long, weary hours on the road? they asked her. 'I thought about plans for the salon,' she said. 'It kept my mind off the aches and pains.' During the early part of the race in Scotland she said she planned the location; a large town, somewhere nice and fashionable along the south coast. When she was being lashed by strong winds and blizzards she worked out the colour scheme; pink and duck-egg blue, with pink overalls for the assistants. And then later still in the walk she thought through all of the other things she would need; hairdryers, wash basins and sterilisers.

Then it was off to the hairdressers herself for a day of pampering and to try to look like a fashionable young woman again rather than a bedraggled teenager who'd just won the 'Race to End All Races'. She had her hair washed and set in the bouffanted style, popular in the early 1960s, at a hairstylists in Penzance, and then she sent her sister Joy off on an errand to buy her some clothes. She opted for a strapless, pink off-the-shoulder number and a pair of white buckskin shoes with three inch stiletto heels. 'I don't care if they hurt,' she said, 'I'm fed up of wearing gym shoes.'

Soon she was appearing in a round of TV adverts. Wendy didn't have any of Dr Barbara Moore's hang-ups about not making money from her walks. She needed every penny to go towards her hairdressing salon. Then she was whisked off in a car to the airport and a flight to London, where she was due to appear on national TV.

THE PEOPLE OF CORNWALL, AND Penzance in particular, had taken Wendy Lewis to their hearts. Local officials queued up to congratulate her and she was showered with gifts. Mr S. T. Peak, the Mayor of Penzance, presented her with a case of silver teaspoons; Alderman Philips, Deputy Mayor of St Ives, presented her with a wooden salad bowl and a wall plaque of Land's End. She was also given an inscribed barometer, a pair of beaten copper earrings, a small signpost pointing to St Ives; Miller's Motorcycle Dealers announced they would be presenting her with a moped. But by far the most unusual gift was that of a sack of coal delivered personally by Edward John Rapson, of Helston, the world champion coal heaver. He had personally carried the hundredweight sack of best nutty-slack on his back from Penzance to Land's End and was rewarded for his efforts with a pint of stout paid for by Billy Butlin. Rapson suggested organising a John O'Groats to Land's End coal heaver's race.

OVER THE NEXT FEW DAYS a rag-bag of Butlin's walkers began to appear at Land's End. Philip Barker from Hampstead, the best dressed man in the race who had worn a bowler hat and city suit all the way, came in a very creditable twenty-first. In keeping with his self-imposed dress code he strolled up to Land's End wearing his morning suit and top hat.

Ivy Bayliss, the fifty year old from West Bromwich who just enjoyed walking, and would walk to and from her sister's house in Dudley each week, came in fourteenth, completing the route in twenty-four days and winning a prize of £50. She had worn a pair of basketball boots completely down at the heel. She was beaten by just three and a quarter hours by the youngest female competitor, sixteen year old Miss J Terry from Folkstone in Kent who won £100.

Lavenia Whippy, the tiny forty-four year old from Fiji who won everyone's hearts with her sunny smile, electric blue tracksuit and parasol, may have been the last walker to cross the border, yet she kept going to finish in twentieth place and win £50. One place ahead of her was fifty-four year old Frances Penman of Kirkintilloch, the woman who planned to have a switched egg every third day. She also won £50. Forty-two year old John Sinclair from Leicester, who had been the joint

Mrs J. Joyce from Clacton-on-Sea came 6th in the woman's race and won £100.

winner of the *News of the World* 'March of the Century', finished in twenty-sixth place.

Custan Travers from Bingley came in thirty-first on a vegetarian diet, Robert Reid from Fairlie in Ayreshire finished in 110th place on his diet of porridge and milk, and sixty-five year old Jim Spence's plan of drinking a pint of liquid a day seemed to work for him when he came in fifty-forth, winning £100 special prize as the oldest competitor.

Wearing race number 167, thirty-three year old John Sellors, a painter and decorator from Wakefield, was so disappointed at not coming first he turned around and walked all the way back to John O'Groats. It took him forty days to cover the 1,782 miles and as he was paying his own expenses he was down to just the small change in his pocket by the time he got there. He was forced to hitch-hike to get home.

The last men home, who were still walking on 23rd March, the cut-off day for the Butlin Race, were thirty-six year old Gerry Prout and twenty-three year old Eddie Mearns. Eddie, a roofer from Edinburgh and Gerry, unemployed from Brighton, had set out on the walk with high hopes of being amongst the prize money but foot trouble began to slow Eddie down when he reached Fort William and he realised he had no chance of catching the leaders. As they made their way through the West Country they were still enjoying their walk and stopping off at a lot of pubs along the way. 'Why carry on?' asked *Daily Mirror* reporter John Edwards. 'When you've come this far,' said Gerry, summing up the attitude of most of Billy Butlin's walkers, 'you may as well finish. I suppose we'll get some satisfaction out of it.'

WHEN WENDY LEWIS ARRIVED BACK home to her native Liverpool she was hailed as a national heroine. On the 19th March 1960 she was cheered by 30,000 football fans and the entire Kop at Anfield when she was presented with a bouquet and a handbag by Liverpool winger Billy Liddell before their two, two draw with Huddersfield Town. Sadly this event had an unpleasant aftermath. The day after Wendy had arrived back from the football ground there was something of a domestic disturbance at home. Her sixteen year old brother John, possibly resenting all of the fuss and attention his sister was getting, became upset and angry. He began shouting, creating a scene and started smashing

Miss M. Byrne from Wallasey came 23rd in the woman's race. Note the sign indicates 1,000 miles to John O'Groats when the actual distance is 874 miles.

windows, and then attacked the washing machine with a pick-axe. Wendy and the rest of the family tried to reason with him and calm him down but he rushed out of the house, swarmed up the drainpipe and onto the roof where there was a stand-off for at least an hour. The police and fire brigade were called and a negotiator was trying to talk him down when suddenly, with a scream, he stumbled, rolled off the roof and fell to the ground. He landed heavily in the next door neighbour's garden and lay very still. The ambulance crew lifted him gently onto a stretcher and he spent the night in hospital. He was shaken and bruised but no bones were broken.

Stroppy younger brothers notwithstanding, Wendy was still the darling of the media. When they asked what she was going to do next she told them that she and her sister Joy were going to walk from London to Rome to present a peace petition to the Pope. They had the necessary sponsorship already in place and they planned to set off just as soon as she'd had time to recover from the Billy Butlin Race.

Back at her home in Frimley, Surrey, when the *Daily Mail* told Dr Barbara Moore about Wendy Lewis's win in the Great Billy Butlin Race she told them she couldn't believe it. 'It doesn't prove a thing,' she said.

Chapter Seventeen: Triumph and Disaster

ON HER TRIUMPHANT RETURN FROM walking from John O'Groats to Land's End, Dr Barbara Moore was at the height of her fame in the United Kingdom and beyond. She'd never enjoyed this amount of celebrity before, not even in the heady days of the 1930s when she was hailed as a motorcycle champion and heroine of Russia. This time her fame was worldwide. 1960 would prove to be her greatest year. A highpoint before her life went into a tailspin.

She herself took no part in the Billy Butlin Walk, yet for the competitors the spectre of her presence was ever there. They knew that had it not been for Dr Babs and the publicity she had generated there would have been no race from John O'Groats and, aside from the lure of the cash prizes, one of the main reasons which prompted competitors to take part was to see how well they could do compared with Dr B.

It would have been interesting if she had taken part in the Billy Butlin Walk. For all she was hailed by the press as the walking wonder of the age, her time of twenty-three days does not compare with Wendy Lewis's winning time of seventeen days and seven hours. A fairer comparison perhaps would be with competitors of a similar age. Here her time is more on par with fifty-four year old Miss Penman from Glasgow who took twenty-three days to complete the course, or sixty-two year old Mrs Nicholas from Camelford in Cornwall who crossed the finishing line at Land's End twenty-six days after leaving John O'Groats and was awarded £100 as the oldest female competitor.

AFTER COMPLETING HER TREK DR Barbara was feted by the media. She was flown to London for TV and press interviews and inundated with offers of sponsorship for other marathon walks. In all of her interviews she was keen to point out that second only to her belief in her strict vegetarian diet was her commitment to a total lack of any form of commercial sponsorship on her walks. She had no manager or agent and, as she told the BBC, she saw her walks as 'a kind of single-handed crusade.'

She was not however, averse to being paid £3,000 by the *People* Sunday newspaper for her serialised life story, yet she took exception to the *Daily Mail's* feature article 'The Walking Wonder' which appeared on 5th February 1960, the day after she arrived at Land's End. She claimed it intimated that she had received sponsorship and profited from her walk.

After her bruising encounters with the legal system in Russia, her numerous short spells in custody, the three year jail sentence in 1933, her hunger strike and eventual release, it would have been reasonable to assume that Dr Moore would steer clear of any form of litigation and all matters of a legal nature in Britain, her new home. This was not the case however. She started proceedings against Associated Newspapers who owned *The Daily Mail* and followed that up with legal action against her eighty-two year-old neighbour, Major-General Sir Kenneth Buchanan, over the right of access to the forecourt area in front of their home at Frimley in Surrey.

If Dr Barbara was at the pinnacle of her fame, one member of her team who wasn't enjoying his winter as he might was Fangio the baby tortoise. When the *Daily Mail's* Herbert Kretzmer interviewed Dr B at her home just after her walk, she was trying to warm the tiny creature up in front of an electric fire while ticking off her husband Harry for not looking after him properly while she was away. Even the broadsheet newspapers came out in support of this four legged veteran of the London to Paris Air Race and the Birmingham to Marble Arch Walk. The *Daily Telegraph* ran a short article with the tag line, 'Hard on Fangio', pointing out that she should have allowed the poor little beast to hibernate through the winter.

AT FOUR O'CLOCK ON THE morning of the 12th of April 1960, Dr Barbara was up on deck of the ocean liner Queen Elizabeth, watching the New York skyline slip by as she sailed into the harbour. She limbered up with a few circuits of the deck then ate a breakfast consisting of tomatoes, lettuce, radish, endives and grated carrot. She landed in America with the intention of walking across the entire continent, 3,200 miles from San Francisco to New York.

The record for walking across North America was set in 1909 when seventy year old Edward Weston covered the then 3,485 miles from Los Angeles to New York in seventy-seven days. In 1926 A. L. Monteverde walked 3,895 miles from San Francisco to New York in seventy-nine days.

As she walked down the gangplank, Dr Barbara was met by a crowd of more than fifty reporters. One of the more mischievous pressmen asked her how she felt about the two men who were setting out from San Francisco, at that very moment, to walk to New York. Dr Moore exploded in a fury.

'This is the first I have heard about them!' she said. 'I wish they would not copy me … the small fry is always trying to follow me.' Dr Moore was always good for copy and an angry Dr Moore even more so. 'My trip was planned a long time in advance and they're a couple of Johnny-come-latelies who rushed over here and started a day ahead of me.' Then she calmed down a little and told them she didn't want her walk to be seen as a race between them. 'I'm not concerned about catching up with them,' she said. Yet it was inevitable that the press would see these two simultaneous attempts as a race to cross the continent.

Yet Dr Moore's vitriol was misplaced. The two men in question were none other than Flight Sergeant Patrick Maloney and Staff Sergeant Mervyn Evans, the paratroopers who had walked from John O'Groats to Land's End in June the previous year and followed it up with walks across the waist of Britain and from Edinburgh to London. The two who, more than anyone else, could be said to have started the marathon walking craze in Britain and without whose efforts, it could be reasonably surmised, Dr Barbara would never have considered using marathon walking as a vehicle to promote herself and her dietary theories. For her to call them 'small fry' and 'Johnny-come-latelies' seems both harsh and unfair.

While Dr Moore was sailing into New York harbour Maloney and Evans were camping in an abandoned fort under the Golden Gate Bridge. They started early with a paddle in a chilly Pacific Ocean then set off walking at six am. Their attempt also far exceeded Dr Barbara's in terms of planning and organisation. They were accompanied by Sergeant Roy Rogers in support, who drove along with them in a small car towing a trailer to prepare their camps and to cook their meals. They planned to cover forty-five miles on the first day and to take several days off the existing record.

Dr Moore flew from New York to San Francisco and started her walk at dawn the next day wearing a red bandanna, leather jacket and crepe-soled walking shoes. In typical Dr Bab's style she got off to a chaotic start. She had arrived on the west coast to find no hotel had been booked for her, and there was no van to carry her supplies. Her sponsor, who she refused to name, had pulled out and she was left with little alternative but to carry on alone or abandon the attempt.

Almost as soon as she set off she was stopped by a traffic cop for jaywalking when she crossed the street against a red light and then walked up the ramp to the Golden Gate Bridge with, instead of against, the traffic. Then she had a brief spat with a spectator who tried to show her a short-cut to the bridge. 'I'll jolly well go my own way,' she told him. Finally she was away, ducking under the turnstile, avoiding the eight pence toll, and heading east along Highway 40.

As the paratroopers and Dr Barbara followed different routes across North America, comparison between the two attempts would be unfair. This did not stop the press reporting that 'Dr Babs Leads' on the 27th of April when they were 530 miles into the walk at Wendover in Utah. Maloney and Evans regained the lead just a few days later.

Trekking without a support vehicle and keeping to her strict vegetarian diet must have been particularly difficult for Dr Barbara. She experimented with eating grass as part of her diet yet whether this was out of necessity or as part of her research was unclear. The grass in the Nevada Dessert, which was little more than sage brush, she described as 'inedible' while the grazing in the Sierra was quite 'tasty'. Her grass eating was so well reported that ranchers would bale up hay and leave it by the roadside with a note saying, 'Dr Moore, stop and have lunch.'

Once again she enjoyed considerable celebrity on her trans-America walk. In Steamboat Springs, Colorado, the Mayor declared a public holiday when she walked into town, and in Denver a crowd of 150,000 turned out to welcome her. She was 'ambushed' by Ute Native Americans wearing their full tribal regalia in Utah, crossed sandy deserts in Missouri and needed snow shoes to navigate the drifts in Colorado. The local ski patrol had to bring out two snow-cats to escort her over the 11,000 foot Rabbit's Ears Pass in the Rocky Mountains which was still blocked by deep snow and closed to all traffic, except of course the intrepid Dr Babs.

On 13th June 1960 at a town called Brazil in Indiana, still some 700 miles out from New York, Dr Barbara stepped off the central reservation of a four lane highway and was hit by a car and knocked to the ground. Fortunately the car was moving very slowly and stopped straight away. Dr Barbara was taken to hospital and kept in overnight. X-rays showed there were no bones broken but she was suffering from some minor abrasions and 'first, second and third degree sunburn.' She was discharged next morning and able to continue her walk.

MEANWHILE MALONEY AND EVANS, STILL marching in their army boots, fatigues and regimental berets were approaching New York. They had maintained a steady pace of four and a half miles per hour right across North America and set a new record of sixty-six days from San Francisco to New York. On 17th June they crossed the Hudson River via the Lincoln Tunnel, emerging into the sunshine at ten in the morning to be met by a crowd of news reporters. They arrived at the British Exhibition being held at the Coliseum and were greeted by a piper playing 'Cock of the North'. Major-General J. N. Carter returned their salute on arrival and they were presented with commemorative exhibition medals by Sir William McFadzean and the chairman of the show Lord Roots. When asked by reporters, they said their feet felt fine even after more than 3,000 miles of walking. Then, being soldiers, they repaired to the Red Lion Inn on the fourth floor of the Coliseum for a well-earned beer.

Dr Moore, commenting on them reaching New York, said, 'Those soldiers and their Route 30. It's as flat as a pancake.'

THE ARRIVAL OF DR BARBARA Moore in New York far overshadowed that of Maloney and Evans in terms of glitter and pizazz. She arrived just two days after Independence Day in an NYPD patrol car in Times Square where a crowd of more than 750 carried her aloft. 'To give her feet a rest,' the people said. Then the Mayor entertained her to a civic reception. She had accepted a lift from the police for the last six miles so she could arrive at a reasonable time and not disappoint the waiting crowd. Next morning she had to back-track and walk the last six miles in order to fully complete her trek.

It may have taken her eighty-five days to reach New York, during which time she lost twenty pounds in weight; she may have missed out on the record; but it was still an outstanding achievement. She had become the first woman to walk across North America.

FOR DR MOORE, THE REMAINDER of 1960 was a blur of marathon walks. She must have woken up some mornings and wondered quite where she was, where she was walking to or from, and even which continent she was on. She followed her trans-America walk with a flight to Australia where she marched from Adelaide to Sydney. Then back to the USA to walk Miami to Toronto Canada, and then in September she arrived in Rome planning to walk 1,800 miles to London in three weeks on a diet of mostly grapes.

By this point marathon treks were beginning to lose their novelty and their newsworthiness. The craze had reached its peak with the Butlin Walk and whilst there was still some interest in taking these walks a stage further and trekking across North America, by late summer and autumn, the public were tiring of Dr Moore and wherever her next mammoth walk turned out to be. In August the *Daily Mail* designated her as their 'bore of the month,' describing her American walk as a 'tetchy stroll' and highlighting her antics when she began pelting US customs officers with fruit. By this point there was a certain amount of bad blood between the *Daily Mail* and Dr Barbara. Less than a year earlier when she was walking Edinburgh to London, reporters from the *Mail* had done their best to assist her in any way they could. They carried her supplies, passed on messages from her husband and let her take rests in their cars. By this point relations had soured and she currently had a court case outstanding against Associated Newspapers, the *Daily Mail's* parent body.

The 'fruit' incident referred to by the *Mail* occurred in early August 1960 when Dr Barbara arrived at San Francisco airport after her walk in Australia and was found to have fruit in her luggage. Customs regulations are strict, preventing the importation of any fruit into California. When officials confiscated Dr Barbara's illegal produce, she had a massive tantrum and began throwing the fruit around the terminal building and at the customs officers. Airline staff had to quickly step in to calm the situation. They rerouted her on a flight to London via Los Angeles, so she wouldn't have to run the gauntlet of US customs again in New York, and provided her with a basket of locally sourced fruit for the rest of her journey.

IN JULY 1961, THE FIRST of Dr Barbara's legal cases came up in the High Court in London. She was suing Associated Newspapers, claiming that the article entitled 'The Walking Wonder' which appeared in the *Daily Mail* on the 5th February 1960, about her arrival in Land's End after her walk from John O'Groats suggested she had made the walk for financial gain.

She did not have any beef with the text of the article itself but was upset that it was surrounded by nineteen small adverts for companies selling fruit and other goods associated with her walk. Adverts such as: 'FYFFITA [bananas] extends sincere congratulations to Dr. Barbara Moore on her fortitude'. Or: 'Jaffa [oranges] congratulate Dr. BARBARA MOORE on the courage and stamina shown on her walks'. The adverts were harmless and inoffensive and this kind of thing (i.e. surrounding a feature article with adverts pertaining to it) was standard commercial practice and still happens today. Yet Dr Moore argued that the presence of these adverts adjacent to the article suggested she had undertaken her walk for commercial gain.

Lawyers for Associated Newspapers claimed this was not the case. Neither the article nor the advertisements were in any way defamatory and she had in fact consented to two of them and had even agreed to photos including Dunlop representatives and a Dunlop van at Land's End. 'Why,' Counsel for the newspaper asked, 'do you think Dunlop sent a van and provided you with shoes?'

'I was naïve,' replied Dr Moore. 'I thought they admired me.'

On the 7th July the jury retired to consider their verdict. They returned after just two hours and found in Dr Moore's favour. They agreed the adverts were defamatory, and they awarded her damages of £1,000. The judge also awarded her half of her legal costs.

The British legal system would never be so kind to her again.

Dr Barbara Moore and her husband Harry had moved to Eastlea Court, Frimley, Surrey in 1958, just as she was starting to recover from her long period of depression. She describes the house as standing 'alone on high ground surrounded by a thick wood.' Eastlea Court was a substantial building divided into flats, approached by a long drive from the road, and with a communal forecourt area which could be accessed by all the flats. The moment she saw it she felt a surge of excitement and they knew that they had to live there. Moving into what was then a semi-rural setting seemed to have been a turning point for her. The depression (or leukaemia) of the previous four years was behind her and she was able to move forward with her life. The following year, 1959, she began her campaign of mammoth walks.

The dispute with her neighbours, eighty-two year old Major-General Sir Kenneth Gray Buchanan and his wife Lady Buchanan, appeared at first sight to be a petty squabble over access to the communal forecourt in front of the house. Dr Barbara wrote to Sir Kenneth, a retired soldier with a long and illustrious military career behind him, and informed him that he no longer had access to the forecourt as she had purchased it. The implication of this was that he no longer had access to get to or from his flat. Matters quickly escalated when Dr Barbara placed a row of flower tubs and large stones across the forecourt to stop Sir Kenneth parking or turning his car there.

Delving a little deeper into this spat between neighbours reveals something of an ulterior motive. Harry Moore bought Flat One Eastlea Court and they moved in. Dr Barbara really wanted Flat Two but they couldn't buy it because Sir Kenneth and Lady Buchanan were already living there. In March 1960 Dr Moore bought the three remaining flats at Eastlea Court plus some of the land, and the forecourt. The only obstacle to her owning the whole property was Sir Kenneth and his wife living in Flat Two. By cutting off his access she believed she had made

156

his flat unsalable and he would have no option but to sell to her. Dr Barbara and Harry would then own the whole property and she could proceed with her plans to build a laboratory and clinic on the site.

Like the time she picked a fight with General Uritzky in Leningrad, once again Dr Barbara made the mistake of going into battle with a formidable opponent. Sir Kenneth, a veteran of the North-West Frontier, a soldier awarded a DSO and mentioned in dispatches, was not going to allow his home to be taken from him by an eccentric Russian dietician, an ineffectual art teacher and a row of plant tubs. He faced her down.

The dispute was not without its lighter moments. Especially when Sir Kenneth's grandchildren chased Harry Moore off the forecourt by firing toy arrows over the plant tubs at him.

It may be a mark of the intransigence of both parties, but particularly of Dr Barbara, that what was really a simple dispute over access could not have been resolved at a local level. Instead the matter came before the High Court in May 1962. After preliminary arguments, the judge, Mr Justice Lawson, ruled that the stones and tubs should be removed from the forecourt while proceedings were taking place and the matter was being decided.

Dr Barbara refused to move the tubs.

The judge explained that this was the ruling of the court and the tubs must be removed.

Dr Barbara again refused to move the tubs.

The judge explained that she must remove the tubs or she would be in contempt of court.

Dr Barbara said she would rather go to prison than remove the tubs.

The judge gave her ten minutes to think about the matter carefully.

After the ten minutes had passed Dr Barbara returned to court. She still refused to move the tubs.

Mr Justice Lawson had no alternative and, reluctantly, he ordered Dr Barbara Moore to prison. He expressed the view that he hoped a short, sharp shock might bring her to her senses.

Short, sharp shocks had never worked with Dr Barbara in the past and they didn't work now. Once she arrived at Holloway Women's Prison, and with echoes of her time in Leningrad jail, she went on hunger strike. 'A hunger strike until death.' She even refused to drink water.

Fasting and hunger strikes had become as much a part of Dr Barbara's life as her marathon walks. It was a strategy which had worked for her before so it shouldn't have come as a surprise that she used the same tactic again. The prison authorities were well aware of how closely the media were following the case. There had already been considerable newspaper coverage with photos of Dr Barbara being marched out of court escorted by a tipstaff on her way to prison. After just a few days of Dr Barbara refusing food, they transferred her to Whittington Hospital at Highgate.

She returned to court a week later yet despite being tearful and visibly upset she still refused to move the tubs. 'I will not take them away,' she said. 'Why should I?'

Dr Moore's plight was distressing to all the other parties involved. The judge didn't want to send her to prison and her husband was in a no-win situation. He was far from happy with the stand she was taking yet seemed powerless to influence her. When Sir Kenneth's counsel suggested that Harry Moore should remove the tubs, Dr Barbara glared and shook a finger at him across the courtroom. He later told reporters, 'My wife wears the trousers in our home and that's the way I want it.'

Mr Justice Lawson had no option but to remand Dr Barbara back to prison.

Two days later there was a breakthrough.

'Dr Babs is Free – and Furious!' was the *Daily Mirror's* banner headline. The tubs had been removed.

The identity of whoever had removed the offending tubs was a mystery. Officially they had been moved by a 'well-wisher'. Dr Babs was in no doubt as to the identity of this supposed 'well-wisher'. The finger of blame pointed directly at Harry. 'I was betrayed,' she told the world's media and she refused a lift home in Harry's car. 'I'd rather walk,' she said. In the event she took a taxi.

Even when they arrived home Harry was still in the firing line. 'I wouldn't betray you,' he said somewhat plaintively.

'I'll get to the bottom of this,' she said, 'then watch out.'

It's hard to not feel a little sorry for poor brow beaten Harry Moore, especially in this case because he truly had not been the one to move the tubs. In a bizarre twist a man from London had taken it on himself to break the impasse and remove the tubs. A short time later, and possibly because poor Harry was still getting the blame, he wrote to Dr Barbara and owned up. She said she would take no further action against him and refused to disclose his name.

DURING THE EPISODE OF THE tubs the judge Mr Justice Lawson told Dr Barbara, 'This comedy must stop.' But the comedy didn't stop. Over the next seven years Dr Barbara's constant petitions, appeals and court appearances reached a farcical level, more like something from A.P. Herbert's *Misleading Cases*.

She appealed her prison sentence for contempt of court. The judge, Lord Justice Sellers pointed out that it was a bit late and pointless to appeal a prison sentence after she had been released. He dismissed her with the warning. 'This court is not to be used as a forum for your grievances.'

It seemed as if legal wrangling had become the new focus of her life, taking over from long-distance walking in the same way as her treks had taken over from motorbike racing. In October 1965 she was unable to attend a court hearing in her case against Sir Kenneth Buchanan, which was still dragging on, because after being up all night, she had collapsed at 5.30 in the morning, apparently from 'overwork'. A doctor had been called. The 'work' in question appeared to be her obsessively going through the arguments and statutes for her legal battles; which seemed to be stacking up.

By 1964 a fresh source of litigation had appeared on the scene, this time against Frimley and Camberley Urban District Council. A new housing development had been built on land behind Eastlea Court but it was impossible for these new homes to be occupied until a sewer had been laid. The only place it could go was across Dr Moore's land. It goes without saying that she refused and seemed delighted that she largely had the council at her mercy. There was also the added complication that any route the sewer would take would have to avoid where she planned to site her laboratory.

In June 1966 the High Court finally ruled against Dr Barbara in the case of Moore versus Buchanan. She had lost and would be unable to replace the plant tubs. The court awarded Sir Kenneth and Lady

Buchanan £250 damages. She appealed the ruling, but this was dismissed. Mr Justice Milmo, presiding, delivered a damning assessment of Dr Barbara's character. 'She is ... an emotional person ... that could and did stage emotional outbursts at will and that was part of her stock in trade to do so when she thought it would further her immediate ends ... [She is] cunning and unscrupulous and wholly unreliable.'

He was hardly more complimentary about Harry. '[He is] under her domination ... [with] neither the ability nor determination to restrain her.'

She failed to stop the local council taking the necessary compulsory purchase measures to enable them to lay the public sewer through the grounds of Eastlea Court, despite taking her objections to the Court of Appeal, the Housing Minister Richard Crossman – she turned up at his house one night at eleven o'clock – and handing in a petition for the Queen at Balmoral.

By the late 1960s these prolonged legal battles were taking their toll on her health, her marriage and her finances. Bankruptcy proceedings were taken against her in 1969 and even these took the usual bizarre twists in keeping with her character. She appealed her bankruptcy, not only with the Court of Appeal in the UK, but also with the European Court in Strasbourg and the International Court of Justice at The Hague. On the eighth of October she sent a telegram to the court requesting an adjournment because she had been attacked by a leopard. The court demanded a doctor's note which she failed to provide, but she later appeared in court with her hands and a foot bandaged.

Harry and Dr Barbara separated and had to leave Eastlea Court. Harry was busy with problems of his own around this time, having been suspended and forced to leave his job as an art teacher at Westgate Secondary School. He had allegedly struck a pupil.

In 1960, when she was at the height of her marathon walking fame, Dr Barbara Moore claimed that her diet and lifestyle would enable her to live to 150 and to have a baby when she was 100. She did not. She died aged seventy-three on the 13th of May 1977, at St Giles Hospital in Camberwell. She had been admitted under the name of Mrs Anne Moore to ensure her anonymity.

She had been found collapsed in her flat a few days earlier and even though there was plenty of food in the kitchen it seemed that she had not been eating or drinking. After her many fasts and two high profile hunger strikes, her lack of eating and drinking finally triggered the kidney failure which killed her.

In her obituary in the *New Vegetarian* Edward Banks said that few people had done quite so much for the true cause of vegetarianism. A sad end, to a 'once internationally known woman.'

Chapter Eighteen: The Legacy

FOR MOST COMPETITORS, THE BILLY Butlin Walk was one of the highlights of that stage of their lives. A crazy, zany, exciting, one-off event. Even if they didn't win any prize money, even if for most of the race they were tired, wet, hungry and footsore, they were glad to have been part of that crowd of 715 footsloggers who raced away from John O'Groats on that cold February evening when the red and green rockets were fired into the air. It pre-dated Andy Warhol's idea of everyone having their fifteen minutes of fame by some eight years, yet for those few weeks in the winter of 1960 they enjoyed being the focus of Britain's, if not the World's, media.

When the walk was over, life quickly returned to normal. The Butlin team went back to their holiday camps and had something of a rush on to get everything ready for the first holiday makers arriving in the spring. The press returned, somewhat gratefully, to Fleet Street while the racers themselves, many of whom had so quickly become household names - John Grundy, Alfred Rozentals, Wendy Lewis, Beryl Randle, David Robinson, James Musgrave - returned to their previous lives. None were to feature in the headlines again.

Jim Musgrave, despite receiving ten proposals of marriage during the walk, stated that he was a confirmed bachelor and planned to remain so. He made one or two public appearances in the aftermath of the race; he opened a local go-cart track, gave a lecture about the walk at a Doncaster store and appealed for funds on behalf of World Refugee Year. After he had paid the £200 which covered his race expenses, he bought himself a push-bike out of his winnings commenting, without any apparent irony, that it would save him a lot of walking when he started back at work. Other than that, he said he planned to use the rest of the cash to help out his family. Musgrave, Grundy and Rosentals all said they would enter again if there was a Butlin Race the following year.

The Amateur Athletics Association quickly reinstated Beryl Randle's amateur status and she remained an active figure in athletics in the Midlands for many years. Even as late as 1995 she was a member of the British Athletics Federation panel under the chairmanship of Robert Reid QC, hearing athlete Diane Modahl's appeal against her four year suspension after testing positive for banned drugs.

Wendy Lewis, who had been such a hit with the people of Cornwall, was back there again only a few months later when she and her sister Joy opened the St Just Fete. Unfortunately the weather was wet so it had to be held in the British Legion Hall. Nonetheless they managed to raise £110 towards the cost of a new church organ. Two months later Wendy announced that she had so fallen in love with Cornwall that she was planning to open her hairdressing salon in Penzance.

'Wendy's Salon' in Albert Street Penzance, was to be an 'ultra-modern' London style beauty salon but with prices that would suit all pockets. The whole family had helped her set it up and she would be running it with sisters Joy and Angel.

Establishing her hairdressing business resulted in a delay before she was able to set out on her Peace Walk to Rome. In January 1962, Angel was left behind in Penzance to keep the salon going, while Wendy and Joy set out on their 1,800 mile trek to Rome, more than twice the distance of John O'Groats to Land's End. They estimated they would be walking for seven weeks. After attending Mass at Westminster Cathedral they sailed from Greenwich to Rotterdam where the walk started. Their route took them through Antwerp, Brussels, Paris, Lyon, Monte Carlo, Pisa and finally Rome. They carried with them several hundred petitions for peace, many from nations around the World, all sealed in a canvas envelope. They hoped for an audience with Pope John XXIII to present their petitions.

DAVID WATHEN, THE SHEEP FARMER from the Scottish Borders who was forced to retire from the race with leg and foot problems close to the end, wrote *The Big Walk*, under the pseudonym 'A. Walker'. *The Big Walk* is a full and detailed account of the race from a participants' point of view with fascinating additional sections by Foot Specialists and Butlin's Race Officials. Published the year after the race, but now sadly out of print, it is the closest to an official account of the race that exists.

David Wathen went on to stand as a Conservative candidate for the Inverness constituency in both 1966 and 1970. He advocated a stance of 'moral strength,' being in favour of both birching and the resumption of capital punishment for murder. He polled 11,961 votes in 1966 and 12,378 in 1970, losing on both occasions to Russell Johnston, the Liberal candidate. David Wathen died in January 2013 at the age of eighty-four.

WHEN, IN LATE 2017 AND early 2018 I began trying to contact any walkers who had competed in the 1960 Billy Butlin Race. I was faced with something of an uphill problem. The race may have been a national sensation at the time, but almost sixty years later it was all but forgotten. What was more, even though most of the participants had kept fit and led active and interesting lives, most of them by that point, like David Wathen, had died.

My starting point was a list of the 1960 contact details for all 138 competitors who had completed the race. I opted for a mass mail shot, hoping that one or two of Butlin's racers would still be contactable at these addresses and might respond. I wrote to each of the finishers, with just one exception: E. Robinson, forty-five at the time of the race and who came in sixty-eighth. He gave his address as an army barracks in Aldershot. Old soldiers are not supposed to die but to simply fade away; even so I couldn't imagine that Mr Robinson, who would have been 102 years old, would still be resident at the Aldershot Barracks. This reduced my mailshot to 137.

In each letter I explained that I was writing about the Butlin Walk and included a reply-paid postcard with tick boxes for: 'Sorry I am unable to help' or 'Yes I have some information which may help'. Many of these 1960 addresses no longer existed and I drove my local post office to distraction. In all I had forty postcards returned marked 'Sorry I am unable to help', twenty-eight letters returned 'address unknown', three helpful phone calls, and an email to tell me about an old Butlin's racer who had gone into a nursing home and subsequently died. Then I struck gold. I was able to talk to Peter Pipe, race number 597 who came forty-fifth; Michael Green, race number 272, one of the youngest competitors in the race who now lives on a farm in Wales; and Alex Dick, the man who fooled his mother into letting him enter the race. He now lives in Canada. We had a lengthy correspondence via email and he was a great fund of information. I also spoke to Ruth Williams, widow of Jack Williams, the woman to whom Dr Barbara Moore said that she would be able to have a baby when she was a hundred. And Duncan Gillies, son of Duncan Gillies, the man who walked till the soles of his shoes wore through. Duncan also shared with me a fantastic fund of information along with some wonderful photos. Shortly before the book was finished I was contacted by David Jones, son of Ben (the Boots) Jones. Again he was able to share with me considerable detail about his father, along with some excellent photos.

BUTLIN'S CAMPS CONTINUED TO BE a top holiday destination through the 1960s until their popularity started to wane in the early 1970s with the coming of cheap package holidays to Spain and the Mediterranean. In 1972, Butlin's became part of the Rank Organisation and in 2000 became part of Bourne Leisure. The facilities and attractions of holiday camps have changed from the early days of 1936, yet they retain the same ethos of everything needed for a holiday being available on one site. Today Butlin's has three camps: Skegness, Bognor Regis and Minehead.

BILLY BUTLIN HIMSELF RETAINED HIS love of newsworthy, eye-catching races and events, especially if they would raise the profile and create publicity for the Butlin's brand. In 1961 he entered the *Daily Express Off-Shore Powerboat Race* in a Hunter class boat, piloted by test pilot Peter Twiss. They were holed off the Nab Tower Lighthouse when they hit a piece of floating debris and only narrowly avoided sinking. Butlin paid for the boat to be repaired and then gave it away to the local Sea Scouts.

In 1969 he entered the *Daily Mail Trans-Atlantic Race*, an event not dissimilar to the 1959 *Daily Mail Cross-Channel Blériot Race* but this time over a much bigger distance. Competitors had to go from the top of the Post Office Tower in London to the top of the Empire State Building in New York in the fastest possible time. Wearing a crash helmet and a morning suit Sir Billy Butlin went via a motorbike driven by an RAF despatch rider to Waterloo, a helicopter to a private airfield in

Hertfordshire, and then a Hawker Siddeley 125 executive jet which flew the polar route to New York. He reached the top of the Empire State in eleven hours, thirty minutes and forty-one point three-five seconds, coming first in his category.

Billy Butlin received his knighthood from the Queen in 1964. He retired from the day to day running of Butlin's in 1968. For a man who had always been so involved and 'hands on' with his holiday camp empire, he did not find it easy to relinquish control and to settle into retirement. 'I had become a consultant to the company,' he said, 'but nobody consulted me.'

In time he did adjust to his new lifestyle. He developed some small business interests in the Channel Islands, where he had moved to avoid crippling tax bills, and continued with his charitable works. Sir Billy Butlin died on 12th June 1980 and is buried in St John's Cemetery on Jersey, in a huge tomb easily seen from the road.

IN THE AFTERMATH OF THE John O'Groats to Land's End race, the Butlin's organisation took a long hard look at the facts and figures. The Secretary of State for Scotland, the Right Honourable Mr John Scott Maclay, stated that the Butlin Race had cost local authorities at least £200 in medical services alone. Butlin countered this by estimating that the press had spent more than £20,000 in Scotland and that as Butlin's vehicles had used 55,000 gallons of fuel, the exchequer would have received thousands of pounds in petrol duty alone.

Butlin used eighty vehicles, 132 staff, paid out £15,000 in prize money and racked up a phone bill of £2,000. He considered this as money well spent because the race was such a success and generated a huge amount of good will and positive publicity for Butlin's Holiday camps. He was also rewarded by a hike in the share price and an increased dividend for investors.

GIVEN THE POPULARITY AND SUCCESSFUL outcome of the race, why were there no Billy Butlin Walks in subsequent years?

During the race itself Butlin seemed quite keen to make it an annual event and was considering modifications for the following year's race. It had been mooted to create different classes next time; categories for walkers, categories for runners and separate classes for athletes with support teams and those without. Also it had been suggested that everyone who entered would have to either prove they had enough money to get themselves home or leave a refundable deposit to prevent the problem of hundreds of walkers dropping out during the first few days and claiming to have no money to pay their fare home. At about the mid-point of the race, Billy Butlin had said there definitely would be another race next year; but by the end his resolve seemed to be slipping. He would see, he said, when asked by the press.

Billy Butlin never stated specifically why he didn't organise a race the following year. It was true that if the financial cost had been very high, then so had the return in publicity and good will. The cost would be likely to increase in future years, yet it is questionable if the publicity value would be as high once it became an annual event. Although he made light of such matters, pulling almost all his staff and vehicles off preparing for the summer season must have placed additional pressures on them as soon as the race was over. Also it must be considered that he had 'chanced his arm' with this race and he'd got away with it. Nobody was killed or badly injured, either by the extreme weather or on the roads. He might not be so lucky next time.

I would suggest however the real reason that Butlin did not make it an annual event was best demonstrated by the redoubtable Mrs Dorothy Scott. She was the forty-six year old widow from Liverpool who caused race organisers such problems in the early stages. She had first set out from John O'Groats in mid-January but followers lost track of her around Glencoe. She entered the Butlin race and there were unfounded reports of her leading the Women's race at one point. Race officials again had difficulty keeping track of her. At one point she was said to have been disqualified, then she was said to be back in the race, then out of the official race but still walking on her own account.

Dorothy Scott had aspirations of being the United Kingdom's answer to Dr Barbara Moore. On 14th June 1960, wearing a sign on her back, 'Walking Round the Coast of England, Scotland and Wales', she set out from Liverpool to walk right around the coast of Britain, a journey of 4,328 miles. She was seen off by the Lord Mayor of Liverpool, Alderman J. Leslie Hughes, and her kit for the walk was provided by a local department store. It was never in doubt that she completed her march. She returned with a file of 383 documents, letters and photos signed by

Lord Mayors and civic officials along the way to prove she had walked where she said. But her return to Liverpool three months later was a non-event.

There were no crowds, no welcome and no civic reception. When she arrived at the department store which had funded her walk, the manager had gone on holiday, the staff weren't expecting her and there was no one available to greet her. Someone gave her a bouquet of flowers, she was treated to lunch in the canteen, and then she caught the bus home where again there was no press, no TV and no crowd of neighbours thronging the street to welcome her back. Dorothy Scott was hugely disappointed and said she felt cheated after all the effort she had put in. 'I have been given the cold shoulder,' she told a reporter from the *Sunday People*. 'I have had a raw deal.'

Dorothy Scott had misread the mood of the nation, whereas Billy Butlin had read it very well. Marathon walking in 1959 and 1960 was a craze, and a short-lived craze at that. It had started in the heady days of summer with Sergeants Maloney and Evans walking from John O'Groats to Land's End in eighteen days. People had quickly jumped on the bandwagon and were soon making their own treks around the country. Dr Barbara Moore rode this wave of public enthusiasm and became the cheerleader for this new obsession, using it to promote her ideas about diet while mostly publicising herself. The Billy Butlin Walk became the climax, with the nation held in thrall as John Grundy, James Musgrave, Wendy Lewis and Beryl Randle fought it out for the men's and women's crown while the plucky also-rans showed what regular folks were capable of. Then it was over. The nation moved on. Crazes have a short shelf-life and this one had run its course. Dorothy Scott and even Dr Moore didn't realise this. Billy Butlin did. He rode the crest of the marathon walking craze, and wisely decided against further races once the fad was over.

TWO MORE QUESTIONS REMAIN TO be answered. Would it be a good idea to ever stage another footrace from John O'Groats to Land's End, like the Billy Butlin Race; and what, if anything, was the legacy of this craze for marathon walking?

As to whether there should be another End to End race, some commentators, citing Health and Safety legislation, have argued that today it would be impossible. There is no foundation for this view any more than there was foundation to the calls by the great and the good back in 1960 demanding that Billy Butlin call off his race. The route would need to be revised a little and road safety issues addressed, but if other major events can be staged on public roads, such as the Tour de France or the Tour de Yorkshire, then an End to End race would not be impossible with adequate preparation and marshalling. Safety issues do not seem to stop Land's End to John O'Groats becoming a favourite challenge for fundraising and sponsored walks.

It is another matter as to whether such a race would be desirable. The Billy Butlin Race was, in the author's view, a one-off event, a high spot which caught the mood of the nation at that specific time. Repeat events would only serve to dilute the magic. Furthermore it would be detrimental to over-organise and regulate such a walk. The End to End is not a national trail like The Pennine Way or The South West Coast Path, which have specific and defined routes. John O'Groats to Land's End has a start point and a finish point and the way a walker chooses to travel between those two points is a matter of personal choice, open to individual interpretation and long may it remain so. However I should stress this is just the author's view. Others may think differently.

Shortly after the Butlin Walk, the travel writer and *Guardian* zoological correspondent John Hillaby set off from Land's End and walked via a mostly green route to John O'Groats. Following his trek he wrote what is arguably the definitive account of the walk, *Journey Through Britain*, and thereby inspired hundreds of others to follow in his footsteps. Whether Hillaby would have made this journey had End to Ending and the Butlin Walk not been so prominent in the years immediately before is a matter for conjecture.

The Billy Butlin Walk, Dr Barbara Moore and the weary footsloggers of the 1959/1960 marathon walking craze did, in the author's view, leave one lasting and important legacy. Prior to 1959, John O'Groats to Land's End was seldom walked. After these events it became firmly fixed in the public consciousness as the quintessential British endurance test. It remains something special: the longest walk you can do in these islands, without doubling back on yourself.

Acknowledgements

It is impossible to research and write a book such as this without a considerable amount of help from many, many different quarters. My grateful thanks go to: Robert Hutchinson for the account of his walks, Alison Fawkner at the Vegetarian Society, Eve Read and Sophie Towne at the History of Advertising Trust, Nick Snow for reading through the manuscript, and the staff at the British Library at both St Pancras and Boston Spa for always being so helpful. Thanks to everyone who responded to my mass mailshot for Butlin Race finishers and special thanks to Peter Pipe, Michael Green and Ruth Williams (wife of Jack Roston Williams) who were all so generous with such valuable information. And grateful thanks to Alex Dick, Duncan Gillies (son of Duncan Gillies) and David Jones (son of Ben the Boots Jones) who were not only generous with unique information but also supplied me with some wonderful photographs.

Finally thanks to my family, friends and the many people who have expressed an interest in this project. Thanks to Rose Drew and all at Stairwell Books, and special thanks to Sarah, my wife, for putting up with a husband obsessed with Billy Butlin, his 1960 race, and all matters John O'Groats to Land's End.

Select Bibliography

Sir Billy Butlin with Peter Dacre, *The Billy Butlin Story 'A Showman to the End*,' London, Robson Books Ltd. 1993.

John Hillaby, *Journey through Britain*, London, Constable, 1997.

Andrew McCloy, *Land' End to John O'Groats*, London, Hodder & Stoughton, 1994.

Barbara Moore-Pataleewa, *I Am A Woman From Soviet Russia*, London, Victor Gollancz Ltd, 1943.

Tom Morris, *The Long Walk*, 2012. https://midlandmasters.files.wordpress.com/2012/09/the-long-walk.pdf accessed 27/02/2018.

Rex North, *The Butlin Story*, London, Jarrolds Publishers Ltd, 1962

Stevenson Pugh, *The Bleriot Anniversary Race*, London, Daily Mail, 1959.

Robin Richards, *LE-JOG-ed, A Mid-lifer's Trek from Land's End to John O'Groats*, Leicester, Matador 2013.

A. Walker, *The Big Walk*, London, Prentice-Hall International Inc, 1961.

J.H. Williams, (Elephant Bill) *Big Charlie*, London, Rupert Hart-Davis, 1959

Picture Credits

AP/Shutterstock:: Pages 7, 17 (Dennis Hart), 63 (Leslie Priest)

David Jones: Pages 78, 95, 133, 139

Beaverbrook Newspapers & from the Butlin's Heritage Collection at the History of Advertising Trust (HAT): Pages 81, 97, 103, 105, 115, 125, 135, 137, 138, 145, 146

Duncan Gillies: Pages 82, 83, 84, 129, 131

John Alex Dick: Pages 121

Other biographies, memoires and history available from Stairwell Books

Mistress	Lorraine White
The Tao of Revolution	Chris Taylor
Margaret Clitherow	John and Wendy Rayne-Davis
Serpent Child	Pat Riley
Looking for Githa	Patricia Riley
The Martyrdoms at Clifford's Tower 1190 and 1537	John Rayne-Davis
A Shadow in My Life	Rita Jerram
Thinking of You Always	Lewis Hill
Tales from a Prairie Journal	Rita Jerram

For further information please contact rose@stairwellbooks.com

www.stairwellbooks.co.uk
@stairwellbooks